Managing Uncertainty

ManageMentor Skill Pack

Lesson From,

Anette Mikes; Nathan Bennett; Hugh Courtney;
David Simchi; William Schmidt; Yehua Wei is;
Martin Reeves; Robert Simons; Gökçe Sargut; Rita
Gunther; Angela Wilkinson; Roland Kupers

Copyright © 2015 ManageMentor Business Management.
Nürnberg, Germany.

A CIP catalogue record for this title is available from the British
Library
ISBN: 1515066576

ISBN-13: 978-1515066576

Printed and bound by
Amazon Media EU S.à r.l. , 5 Rue Plaetis, L-2338 Luxemburg.

Amazon.com, Inc.; Seattle, WA 98108-1226, USA

CONTENTS

ACKNOWLEDGMENTS

- *Robert S. Kaplan* is a Baker Foundation Professor at Harvard Business School and the cocreator of the Balanced Scorecard management system.

- *Anette Mikes* is an assistant professor at Harvard Business School

- *Nathan Bennett* is a professor at Georgia State University's Robinson College of Business. G. James Lemoine is a doctoral candidate at Georgia Institute of Technology'

- *Hugh Courtney* is the dean and a professor of international business and strategy at Northeastern University's D'Amore-McKim School of Business and a former consultant at McKinsey & Company. Dan Lovallo is a professor of business strategy at the University of Sydney and a senior adviser to McKinsey & Company. Carmina Clarke is a senior manager at Macquarie Group.

- *David Simchi-Levi* is a professor of engineering systems at the Operations Research Center of the Massachusetts Institute of Technology.

- *William Schmidt* is an assistant professor at Cornell University's Johnson Graduate School of Management.

- *Yehua Wei* is an assistant professor at Duke University's Fuqua School of Business.

- *Michael E. Porter* is the Bishop William Lawrence University Professor at Harvard University. He is a frequent contributor to Harvard Business Review and a six-time McKinsey Award winner. Mark R. Kramer cofounded FSG, a global social impact consulting firm, with Professor Porter and is its managing director.

- *Martin Reeves* and Mike Deimler are partners at the Boston Consulting Group, global consultancy with headquarters in Massachusetts.

- *Robert Simons* is the Charles M. Williams Professor of Business dministration at Harvard Business School. This article is adapted from his book Seven Strategy Questions: A Simple Approach for Better Execution (Harvard Business Review Press, 2010).

- *Gökçe Sargut* is an assistant professor at Governors State University, in University Park, Illinois. His research focuses on strategy and structural change in creative industries.

- *Rita Gunther McGrath* is a professor at Columbia Business School. She researches strategy and innovation in volatile environments.

- *Angela Wilkinson* is the program director of the Futures Directorate at Oxford University's Smith School of Enterprise and the Environment. She spent nearly a decade on Shell's corporate scenario team.

- *Roland Kupers*, an associate fellow at Oxford University, is a consultant who has written about complexity and futures. He was formerly a senior executive at Shell and at AT&T. He is the coauthor of a forthcoming book on the history of Shell scenarios.

CHAPTER 1

Managing Risks: A New Framework

Smart companies match their approach to the nature of the threats they face. by Robert S. Kaplan and Anette Mikes

When Tony Hayward became CEO of BP, in 2007, he vowed to make safety his top priority. Among the new rules he instituted were the requirements that all employees use lids on coffee cups while walking and refrain from texting while driving. Three years later, on Hayward's watch, the *Deepwater Horizon* oil rig exploded in the Gulf of Mexico, causing one of the worst man-made disasters in history. A U.S. investigation commission attributed the disaster to management failures that crippled "the ability of individuals involved to identify the risks they faced and to properly evaluate, communicate, and address them."

Hayward's story reflects a common problem, Despite all the rhetoric and money invested in it, risk management is too often treated as a compliance issue that can be solved by drawing up lots of rules and making sure that all employees follow them. Many such rules, of course, are sensible and do reduce some risks that could severely damage a company. But rules-based risk management will not diminish either the likelihood or the impact of a disaster such as Deepwater Horizon, just as it did not prevent the failure of many financial institutions during the 2007–2008 credit crisis.

In this article, we present a new categorization of risk that allows executives to tell which risks can be managed through a rules-based model and which require alternative approaches. We examine the individual and organizational challenges inherent in generating open, constructive discussions about managing the risks related to strategic choices and argue that companies need to anchor these discussions in their strategy formulation and implementation processes. We conclude by looking at how organizations can identify and prepare for nonpreventable risks that arise externally to their strategy and operations.

Managing Risk: Rules or Dialogue?

The first step in creating an effective risk-management system is to understand the qualitative distinctions among the types of risks that organizations face. Our field research shows that risks fall into one of three categories. Risk events from any category can be fatal to a company's strategy and even to its survival.

Category I: Preventable risks. These are internal risks, arising from within the organization, that are controllable and ought to be eliminated or avoided. Examples are the risks from employees' and managers' unauthorized, illegal, unethical, incorrect, or inappropriate actions and the risks from breakdowns in routine operational processes. To be sure, companies should have a zone of tolerance for defects or errors that would not cause severe damage to the enterprise and for which achieving complete avoidance would be too costly. But in general, companies should seek to eliminate these risks since they get no strategic benefits from taking them on. A rogue trader or an employee bribing a local official may produce some short-term profits for the firm, but over time such actions will diminish the company's value.

This risk category is best managed through active prevention: monitoring operational processes and guiding people's behaviors and decisions toward desired norms. Since considerable literature already exists on the rules-based compliance approach, we refer interested readers to the section "Identifying and Managing Preventable Risks" in lieu of a full discussion of best practices here.

Category II: Strategy risks. A company voluntarily accepts some risk in order to generate superior returns from its strategy. A bank assumes credit risk, for example, when it lends money; many companies take on risks through their research and development activities.

Strategy risks are quite different from preventable risks because they are not inherently undesirable. A strategy with high expected returns generally requires the company to take on significant risks, and managing those risks is a key driver in capturing the potential gains. BP accepted the high risks of drilling several miles below the surface of the Gulf of Mexico because of the high value of the oil and gas it hoped to extract.

Strategy risks cannot be managed through a rules-based control model. Instead, you need a riskmanagement system designed to reduce the probability that the assumed risks actually materialize and to improve the company's ability to manage or contain the risk events should they occur. Such a system would not stop companies from undertaking risky ventures; to the contrary, it would enable companies to take on higher-risk, higher-reward ventures than could competitors with less effective risk management.

Category III: External risks. Some risks arise from events outside the company and are beyond its influence or control. Sources of these risks include natural and political disasters and major macroeco nomic shifts. External risks require yet another approach. Because companies cannot prevent such events from occurring, their management must focus on identification (they tend to be obvious in hindsight) and mitigation of their impact.

Companies should tailor their risk-management processes to these different categories. While a compliance-based approach is effective for managing preventable risks, it is wholly inadequate for strategy risks or external risks, which require a fundamentally different approach based on open and explicit risk discussions. That, however, is easier said than done; extensive behavioral and organizational research has shown that individuals have strong cognitive biases that discourage them from thinking about and discussing risk until it's too late.

Why Risk Is Hard to Talk About Multiple studies have found that people overestimate their ability to influence events that, in fact, are heavily determined by chance. We tend to be *overconfident* about the accuracy of our forecasts and risk assessments and far too narrow in our assessment of the range of outcomes that may occur.

We also *anchor our estimates* to readily available evidence despite the known danger of making linear extrapolations from recent history to a highly uncertain and variable future. We often compound this problem with a *confirmation bias,* which drives us to favor information that supports our positions (typically successes) and suppress information that contradicts them (typically failures). When events depart from our expectations, we tend to *escalate commitment,* irrationally directing even more resources to our failed course of action—throwing good money after bad.

Organizational biases also inhibit our ability to discuss risk and failure. In particular, teams facing uncertain conditions often engage in *groupthink*: Once a course of action has gathered support within a group, those not yet on board tend to suppress their objections—however valid—and fall in line. Groupthink is especially likely if the team is led by an overbearing or overconfident manager who wants to minimize conflict, delay, and challenges to his or her authority.

Collectively, these individual and organizational biases explain why so many companies overlook or misread ambiguous threats. Rather than mitigating risk, firms actually incubate risk through the *normalization of deviance,* as they learn to tolerate apparently minor failures and defects and treat early warning signals as false alarms rather than alerts to imminent danger.

Managing Risks: A New Framework

Effective risk-management processes must counteract those biases. "Risk mitigation is painful, not a natural act for humans to perform," says Gentry Lee, the chief systems engineer at Jet Propulsion Laboratory (JPL), a division of the U.S. National Aeronautics and Space Administration. The rocket scientists on JPL project teams are top graduates from elite universities, many of whom have never experienced failure at school or work. Lee's biggest challenge in establishing a new risk culture at JPL was to get project teams to feel comfortable thinking and talking about what could go wrong with their excellent designs.

Rules about what to do and what not to do won't help here. In fact, they usually have the opposite effect, encouraging a checklist mentality that inhibits challenge and discussion. Managing strategy risks and external risks requires very different approaches. We start by examining how to identify and mitigate strategy risks.

Managing Strategy Risks

Over the past 10 years of study, we've come across three distinct approaches to managing strategy risks. Which model is appropriate for a given firm depends largely on the context in which an organization operates. Each approach requires quite different structures and roles for a risk-management function, but all three encourage employees to challenge existing assumptions and debate risk information. Our finding that "one size does not fit all" runs counter to the efforts of regulatory authorities and professional associations to standardize the function.

Independent experts. Some organizations—particularly those like JPL that push the envelope of technological innovation—face high intrinsic risk as they pursue long, complex, and expensive product-development projects. But since much of the risk arises from coping with known laws of nature, the risk changes slowly over time. For these organizations, risk management can be handled at the project level.

JPL, for example, has established a risk review board made up of independent technical experts whose role is to challenge project engineers' design, risk-assessment, and risk-mitigation decisions. The experts ensure that evaluations of risk take place periodically throughout the product-development cycle. Because the risks are relatively unchanging, the review board needs to meet only once or twice a year, with the project leader and the head of the review board meeting quarterly.

The risk review board meetings are intense, creating what Gentry Lee calls "a culture of intellectual confrontation." As board member Chris Lewicki says, "We tear each other apart, throwing stones and giving very critical commentary about everything that's going on." In the process, project engineers see their work from another perspective. "It lifts their noses away from the grindstone," Lewicki adds.

The meetings, both constructive and confrontational, are not intended to inhibit the project team from pursuing highly ambitious missions and designs. But they force engineers to think in advance about how they will describe and defend their design decisions and whether they have sufficiently considered likely failures and defects. The board members, acting as devil's advocates, counterbalance the engineers' natural overconfidence, helping to avoid escalation of commitment to projects with unacceptable levels of risk.

At JPL, the risk review board not only promotes vigorous debate about project risks but also has authority over budgets. The board establishes cost and time reserves to be set aside for each project component according to its degree of innovativeness. A simple extension from a prior mission would require a 10% to 20% financial reserve, for instance, whereas an entirely new component that had yet to work on Earth—much less on an unexplored planet—could require a 50% to 75% contingency. The reserves ensure that when problems inevitably arise, the project team has access to the money and time needed to resolve them without jeopardizing the launch date. JPL takes the estimates seriously; projects have been deferred or canceled if funds were insufficient to cover recommended reserves.

Facilitators. Many organizations, such as traditional energy and water utilities, operate in stable technological and market environments, with relatively predictable customer demand. In these situations risks stem largely from seemingly unrelated operational choices across a complex organization that accumulate gradually and can remain hidden for a long time.

Since no single staff group has the knowledge to perform operational-level risk management across diverse functions, firms may deploy a relatively small central risk-management group that collects information from operating managers. This increases managers' awareness of the risks that have been taken on across the organization and provides decision makers with a full picture of the company's risk profile.

We observed this model in action at Hydro One, the Canadian electricity company. Chief risk officer John Fraser, with the explicit backing of the CEO, runs dozens of workshops each year at which employees from all levels and functions identify and rank the principal risks they see to the company's strategic objectives. Employees use an anonymous voting technology to rate each risk, on a scale of 1 to 5, in terms of its impact, the likelihood of occurrence, and the strength of existing controls. The rankings are discussed in the workshops, and employees are empowered to voice and debate their risk perceptions. The group ultimately develops a consensus view that gets recorded on a visual risk map, recommends action plans, and designates an "owner" for each major risk.

Hydro One strengthens accountability by linking capital allocation and budgeting decisions to i identified risks. The corporate-level capital-planning process allocates hundreds of millions of dollars, principally to projects that reduce risk effectively and efficiently. The risk group draws upon technical experts to challenge line engineers' investment plans and risk assessments and to provide independent expert oversight to the resource allocation process. At the annual capital allocation meeting, line managers have to defend their proposals in front of their peers and top executives. Managers want their projects to attract funding in the risk-based capital planning process, so they learn to overcome their bias to hide or minimize the risks in their areas of accountability.

Embedded experts. The financial services industry poses a unique challenge because of the volatile dynamics of asset markets and the potential impact of decisions made by decentralized traders and investment managers. An investment bank's risk profile can change dramatically with a single deal or major market movement. For such companies, risk management requires embedded experts within the organization to continuously monitor and influence the business's risk profile, working side by side with the line managers whose activities are generating new ideas, innovation, and risks and, if all goes well, profits.

JP Morgan Private Bank adopted this model in 2007, at the onset of the global financial crisis. Risk managers, embedded within the line organization, report to both line executives and a centralized, independent riskmanagement function. The face-to-face contact with line managers enables the marketsavvy risk managers to continually ask "what if" questions, challenging the assumptions of portfolio managers and forcing them to look at different scenarios. Risk managers assess how proposed trades affect the risk of the entire investment portfolio, not only under normal circumstances but also under times of extreme stress, when the correlations of returns across different asset classes escalate. "Portfolio managers come to me with three trades, and the [risk] model may say that all three are adding to the same type of risk," explains Gregoriy Zhikarev, a risk manager at JP Morgan. "Nine times out of 10 a manager will say, 'No, that's not what I want to do.' Then we can sit down and redesign the trades."

The chief danger from embedding risk managers within the line organization is that they "go native," aligning themselves with the inner circle of the business unit's leadership team—becoming deal makers rather than deal questioners. Preventing this is the responsibility of the company's senior risk officer and—ultimately—the CEO, who sets the tone for a company's risk culture.

Avoiding the Function Trap

Even if managers have a system that promotes rich discussions about risk, a second cognitivebehavioral trap awaits them. Because many strategy risks (and some external risks) are quite predictable—even familiar—companies tend to label and compartmentalize them, especially along business function lines. Banks often manage what they label "credit risk," "market risk," and "operational risk" in separate groups. Other companies compartmentalize the management of "brand risk," "reputation risk," "supply chain risk," "human resources risk," "IT risk," and "financial risk."

Such organizational silos disperse both information and responsibility for effective risk management. They inhibit discussion of how different risks interact. Good risk discussions must be not only confrontational but also integrative. Businesses can be derailed by a combination of small events that reinforce one another in unanticipated ways.

Managers can develop a companywide risk perspective by anchoring their discussions in strategic planning, the one integrative process that most wellrun companies already have. For example, Infosys, the Indian IT services company, generates risk discussions from the Balanced Scorecard, its management tool for strategy measurement and communication. "As we asked ourselves about what risks we should be looking at," says M.D. Ranganath, the chief risk officer, "we gradually zeroed in on risks to business objectives specified in our corporate scorecard."

In building its Balanced Scorecard, Infosys had identified "growing client relationships" as a key objective and selected metrics for measuring progress, such as the number of global clients with annual billings in excess of $50 million and the annual percentage increases in revenues from large clients. In looking at the goal and the performance metrics together, management realized that its strategy had introduced a new risk factor: client default. When Infosys's business was based on numerous small clients, a single client default would not jeopardize the company's strategy. But a default by a $50 million client would present a major setback. Infosys began to monitor the credit default swap rate of every large client as a leading indicator of the likelihood of default. When a client's rate increased, Infosys would accelerate collection of receivables or request progress payments to reduce the likelihood or impact of default.

To take another example, consider Volkswagen do Brasil (subsequently abbreviated as VW), the Brazilian subsidiary of the German carmaker. VW's risk-management unit uses the company's strategy map as a starting point for its dialogues about risk. For each objective on the map, the group identifies the risk events that could cause VW to fall short of that objective. The team then generates a Risk Event Card for each risk on the map, listing the practical effects of the event on operations, the probability of occurrence, leading indicators, and potential actions for mitigation. It also identifies who has primary accountability for managing the risk. (See the section "The Risk Event Card.") The risk team then presents a high-level summary of results to senior management.

Beyond introducing a systematic process for identifying and mitigating strategy risks, companies also need a risk oversight structure. Infosys uses a dual structure: a central risk team that identifies general strategy risks and establishes central policy, and specialized functional teams that design and monitor policies and controls in consultation with local business teams. The decentralized teams have the authority and expertise to help the business lines respond to threats and changes in their risk profiles, escalating only the exceptions to the central risk team for review. For example, if a client relationship manager wants to give a longer credit period to a company whose credit risk parameters are high, the functional risk manager can send the case to the central team for review.

These examples show that the size and scope of the risk function are not dictated by the size of the organization. Hydro One, a large company, has a relatively small risk group to generate risk awareness and communication throughout the firm and to advise the executive team on risk-based resource allocations. By contrast, relatively small companies or units, such as JPL or JP Morgan Private Bank, need multiple project-level review boards or teams of embedded risk managers to apply domain expertise to assess the risk of business decisions. And Infosys, a large company with broad operational and strategic scope, requires a strong centralized riskmanagement function as well as dispersed risk managers who support local business decisions and facilitate the exchange of information with the centralized risk group.

Managing the Uncontrollable

External risks, the third category of risk, cannot typically be reduced or avoided through the approaches used for managing preventable and strategy risks. External risks lie largely outside the company's control; companies should focus on identifying them, assessing their potential impact, and figuring out how best to mitigate their effects should they occur. Some external risk events are sufficiently imminent that managers can manage them as they do their strategy risks. For example, during the economic slowdown after the global financial crisis, Infosys identified a new risk related to its objective of developing a global workforce: an upsurge in protectionism, which could lead to tight restrictions on work visas and permits for foreign nationals in several OECD countries where Infosys had large client engagements. Although protectionist legislation is technically an external risk since it's beyond the company's control, Infosys treated it as a strategy risk and created a Risk Event Card for it, which included a new risk indicator: the number and percentage of its employees with dual citizenships or existing work permits outside India. If this number were to fall owing to staff turnover, Infosys's global strategy might be jeopardized. Infosys therefore put in place recruiting and retention policies that mitigate the consequences of this external risk event.

Most external risk events, however, require a different analytic approach either because their probability of occurrence is very low or because managers find it difficult to envision them during their normal strategy processes. We have identified several different sources of external risks:

- *Natural and economic disasters with immediate impact.* These risks are predictable in a general way, although their timing is usually not (a large earthquake will hit someday in California, but there is no telling exactly where or when). They may be anticipated only by relatively weak signals. Examples include natural disasters such as the 2010 Icelandic volcano eruption that closed European airspace for a week and economic disasters such as the bursting of a major asset price bubble. When these risks occur, their effects are typically drastic and immediate, as we saw in the disruption from the Japanese earthquake and tsunami in 2011.

- *Geopolitical and environmental changes with long-term impact.* These include political shifts such as major policy changes, coups, revolutions, and wars; long-term environmental changes such as global warming; and depletion of critical natural resources such as fresh water.

- *Competitive risks with medium-term impact.* These include the emergence of disruptive technologies (such as the internet, smartphones, and bar codes) and radical strategic moves by industry players (such as the entry of Amazon into book retailing and Apple into the mobile phone and consumer electronics industries).

Companies use different analytic approaches for each of the sources of external risk.

Tail-risk stress tests. Stress-testing helps companies assess major changes in one or two specific variables whose effects would be major and imme diate, although the exact timing is not forecastable. Financial services firms use stress tests to assess, for example, how an event such as the tripling of oil prices, a large swing in exchange or interest rates, or the default of a major institution or sovereign country would affect trading positions and investments.

CATEGORY 1 **Preventable Risks**	CATEGORY 2 **Strategy Risks**	CATEGORY 3 **External Risks**
Risks arising from within the company that generate no strategic benefits	Risks taken for superior strategic returns	External, uncontrollable risks
RISK MITIGATION OBJECTIVE		
Avoid or eliminate occurrence cost-effectively	Reduce likelihood and impact cost-effectively	Reduce impact cost-effectively should risk event occur
CONTROL MODEL		
Integrated culture-and-compliance model: Develop mission statement; values and belief systems; rules and boundary systems; standard operating procedures; internal controls and internal audit	Interactive discussions about risks to strategic objectives drawing on tools such as: · Maps of likelihood and impact of identified risks · Key risk indicator (KRI) scorecards Resource allocation to mitigate critical risk events	"Envisioning" risks through: · Tail-risk assessments and stress testing · Scenario planning · War-gaming
ROLE OF RISK-MANAGEMENT STAFF FUNCTION		
Coordinates, oversees, and revises specific risk controls with internal audit function	Runs risk workshops and risk review meetings Helps develop portfolio of risk initiatives and their funding Acts as devil's advocates	Runs stress-testing, scenario-planning and war-gaming exercises with management team Acts as devil's advocates
RELATIONSHIP OF THE RISK-MANAGEMENT FUNCTION TO BUSINESS UNITS		
Acts as independent overseers	Acts as independent facilitators, independent experts, or embedded experts	Complements strategy team or serves as independent facilitators of "envisioning" exercises

The benefits from stress-testing, however, depend critically on the assumptions—which may themselves be biased—about how much the variable in question will change. The tail-risk stress tests of many banks in 2007–2008, for example, assumed a worst-case scenario in which U.S. housing prices leveled off and remained flat for several periods. Very few companies thought to test what would happen if prices began to decline—an excellent example of the tendency to anchor estimates in recent and readily available data. Most companies extrapolated from recent U.S. housing prices, which had gone several decades without a general decline, to develop overly optimistic market assessments.

Scenario planning. This tool is suited for longrange analysis, typically five to 10 years out. Originally developed at Shell Oil in the 1960s, scenario analysis is a systematic process for defining the plausible boundaries of future states of the world. Participants examine political, economic, technological, social, regulatory, and environmental forces and select some number of drivers—typically four—that would have the biggest impact on the company. Some companies explicitly draw on the expertise in their advisory boards to inform them about significant trends, outside the company's and industry's day-today focus, that should be considered in their scenarios.

For each of the selected drivers, participants estimate maximum and minimum anticipated values over five to 10 years. Combining the extreme About half tend to be implausible and are discarded; participants then assess how their firm's strategy would perform in the remaining scenarios. If managers see that their strategy is contingent on a generally optimistic view, they can modify it to accommodate pessimistic scenarios or develop plans for how they would change their strategy should early indicators show an increasing likelihood of events turning against it.

War-gaming. War-gaming assesses a firm's vulnerability to disruptive technologies or changes in competitors' strategies. In a war-game, the company assigns three or four teams the task of devising plausible near-term strategies or actions that existing or potential competitors might adopt during the next one or two years—a shorter time horizon than that of scenario analysis. The teams then meet to examine how clever competitors could attack the company's strategy. The process helps to overcome the bias of leaders to ignore evidence that runs counter to their current beliefs, including the possibility of actions that competitors might take to disrupt their strategy.

Companies have no influence over the likelihood of risk events identified through methods such as tail-risk testing, scenario planning, and war-gaming. But managers can take specific actions to mitigate their impact. Since moral hazard does not arise for nonpreventable events, companies can use insurance or hedging to mitigate some risks, as an airline does when it protects itself against sharp increases in fuel prices by using financial derivatives. Another option is for firms to make investments now to avoid much higher costs later. For instance, a manufacturer with facilities in earthquake-prone areas can increase its construction costs to protect critical facilities against severe quakes. Also, companies exposed to different but comparable risks can cooperate to mitigate them. For example, the IT data centers of a university in North Carolina would be vulnerable to hurricane risk while those of a comparable university on the San Andreas Fault in California would be vulnerable to earthquakes. The likelihood that both disasters would happen on the same day is small enough that the two universities might choose to mitigate their risks by backing up each other's systems every night.

The Leadership Challenge

Managing risk is very different from managing strategy. Risk management focuses on the negative—threats and failures rather than opportunities and successes. It runs exactly counter to the "can do" culture most leadership teams try to foster when implementing strategy. And many leaders have a tendency to discount the future; they're reluctant to spend time and money now to avoid an uncertain future problem that might occur down the road, on someone else's watch. Moreover, mitigating risk typically involves dispersing resources and diversifying investments, just the opposite of the intense focus of a successful strategy. Managers may find it antithetical to their culture to champion processes that identify the risks to the strategies they helped to formulate.

For those reasons, most companies need a separate function to handle strategy- and external-risk management. The risk function's size will vary from company to company, but the group must report directly to the top team. Indeed, nurturing a close relationship with senior leadership will arguably be its most critical task; a company's ability to weather storms depends very much on how seriously executives take their risk-management function when the sun is shining and no clouds are on the horizon.

That was what separated the banks that failed in the financial crisis from those that survived. The failed companies had relegated risk management to a compliance function; their risk managers had limited access to senior management and their boards of directors. Further, executives routinely ignored risk managers' warnings about highly leveraged and concentrated positions. By contrast, Goldman Sachs and JPMorgan Chase, two firms that weathered the financial crisis well, had strong internal risk-management functions and leadership teams that understood and managed the companies' multiple risk exposures. Barry Zubrow, chief risk officer at JP Morgan Chase, told us, "I may have the title, but [CEO] Jamie Dimon is the chief risk officer of the company."

Risk management is nonintuitive; it runs counter to many individual and organizational biases. Rules and compliance can mitigate some critical risks but not all of them. Active and cost-effective risk management requires managers to think systematically about the multiple categories of risks they face so that they can institute appropriate processes for each. These processes will neutralize their managerial bias of seeing the world as they would like it to be rather than as it actually is or could possibly become.

Identifying and Managing Preventable Risks

Companies cannot anticipate every circumstance or conflict of interest that an employee might encounter.

Thus, the first line of defense against preventable risk events is to provide guidelines clarifying the company's goals and values.

The Mission A well-crafted mission statement articulates the organization's fundamental purpose, serving as a "true north" for all employees to follow. The first sentence of Johnson & Johnson's renowned credo, for instance, states, "We believe our first responsibility is to the doctors, nurses and patients, to mothers and fathers, and all others who use our products and services," making clear to all employees whose interests should take precedence in any situation. Mission statements should be communicated to and understood by all employees.

The Values Companies should articulate the values that guide employee behavior toward principal stakeholders, including customers, suppliers, fellow employees, communities, and shareholders. Clear value statements help employees avoid violating the company's standards and putting its reputation and assets at risk.

The Boundaries A strong corporate culture clarifies what is not allowed. An explicit definition of boundaries is an effective way to control actions. Consider that nine of the Ten Commandments and nine of the first 10 amendments to the U.S. Constitution (commonly known as the Bill of Rights) are written in negative terms. Companies need corporate codes of business conduct that prescribe behaviors relating to conflicts of interest, antitrust issues, trade secrets and confidential information, bribery, discrimination, and harassment. Of course, clearly articulated statements of mission, values, and boundaries don't in themselves ensure good behavior. To counter the dayto-day pressures of organizational life, top managers must serve as role models and demonstrate that they mean what they say. Companies must institute strong internal control systems, such as the segregation of duties and an active whistle-blowing program, to reduce not only misbehavior but also temptation. A capable and independent internal audit department tasked with continually checking employees' compliance with internal controls and standard operating processes also will deter employees from violating company procedures and policies and can detect violations when they do occur.

The Risk Event Card

VW do Brasil uses risk event cards to assess its strategy risks. First, managers document the risks associated with achieving each of the company's strategic objectives. For each identified risk, managers create a risk card that lists the practical effects of the event's occurring on operations. Below is a sample card looking at the effects of an interruption in deliveries, which could jeopardize VW's strategic objective of achieving a smoothly functioning supply chain.

Understanding the Three Categories of Risk

STRATEGIC OBJECTIVE	RISK EVENT	OUTCOMES	RISK INDICATORS	LIKELIHOOD/ CONSEQUENCES	MANAGEMENT CONTROLS	ACCOUNTABLE MANAGER
Guarantee reliable and competitive supplier-to-manufacturer processes	Interruption of deliveries	Overtime Emergency freight Quality problems Production losses	Critical items report Late deliveries Incoming defects Incorrect component shipments	5 4 3 2 1 X 1 2 3 4 5	Hold daily supply chain meeting with logistics, purchasing, and QA Monitor suppliers' tooling to detect deterioration Risk mitigation initiative: Upgrade suppliers' tooling Risk mitigation initiative: Identify the key supply chain executive at each critical supplier	Mr. O. Manuel, director of manufacturing logistics

The risks that companies face fall into three categories, each of which requires a different risk-management approach. Preventable risks, arising from within an organization, are monitored and controlled through rules, values, and standard compliance tools. In contrast, strategy risks and external risks require distinct processes that encourage managers to openly

discuss risks and find cost-effective ways to reduce the likelihood of risk events ormitigate their consequences

The Risk Report Card

VW do Brasil summarizes its strategy risks on a Risk Report Card organized by strategic objectives (excerpt below). Managers can see at a glance how many of the identified risks for each objective are critical and require attention or mitigation. For instance, VW identified 11 risks associated with achieving the goal "Satisfy the customer's expectations." Four of the risks were critical, but that was an improvement over the previous quarter's assessment. Managers can also monitor progress on risk management across the company.

STRATEGIC OBJECTIVE	ASSESSED RISKS	CRITICAL RISKS	TREND
Achieve market share growth	4	1	⟺
Satisfy the customer's expectations	11	4	⬆
Improve company image	13	1	⟺
Develop dealer organization	4	2	⟺
Guarantee customer-oriented innovations management	5	2	⬇
Achieve launch management efficiency	1	0	⟺
Increase direct processes efficiency	4	1	⟺
Create and manage a robust production volume strategy	2	1	⬇
Guarantee reliable and competitive supplier-to-manufacturer processes	9	3	⟺
Develop an attractive and innovative product portfolio	4	2	⬇

The Idea in Brief

For all the rhetoric about its importance and the money invested in it, risk management is too often treated as a compliance issue.

A rules-based risk-management system may work well to align values and control employee behavior, but it is unsuitable for managing risks inherent in a company's strategic choices or the risks posed by major disruptions or changes in the external environment. Those types of risk require systems aimed at generating discussion and debate.

For strategy risks, companies must tailor approaches to the scope of the risks involved and their rate of change. Though the risk-management functions may vary from company to company, all such efforts must be anchored in corporate strategic-planning processes.

To manage major external risks outside the company's control, companies can call on tools such as war-gaming and scenario analysis. The choice of approach depends on the immediacy of the potential risk's impact and whether it arises from geopolitical, environmental, economic, or competitive changes.

CHAPTER 2
What VUCA Really Means for You

It's become a trendy managerial acronym: VUCA, short for *volatility, uncertainty, complexity,* and *ambiguity,* and a catchall for "Hey, it's crazy out there!" It's also misleading: VUCA conflates four distinct types of challenges that demand four distinct types of responses. That makes it difficult to know how to approach a challenging situation and easy to use VUCA as a crutch, a way to throw off the hard work of strategy and planning—after all, you can't prepare for a VUCA world, right?

Actually, you can. Here is a guide to identifying, getting ready for, and responding to events in each of the four VUCA categories.

1. Complexity

- **Characteristics:** The situation has many interconnected parts and variables. Some information is available or can be predicted, but the volume or nature of it can be overwhelming to process.
- **Example:** You are doing business in many countries, all with unique regulatory environments, tariffs, and cultural values.
- **Approach:** Restructure, bring on or develop specialists, and build up resources adequate to address the complexity.

2. Ambiguity

- **Characteristics:** Causal relationships are completely unclear. No precedents exist; you face "unknown unknowns."
- **Example:** You decide to move into immature or emerging markets or to launch products outside your core competencies.
- **Approach:** Experiment. Understanding cause and effect requires generating hypotheses and testing them. Design your experiments so that lessons learned can be broadly applied.

3. Volatility

- **Characteristics:** The challenge is unexpected or unstable and may be of unknown duration, but it's not necessarily hard to understand; knowledge about it is often available.
- **Example:** Prices fluctuate after a natural disaster takes a supplier off-line.
- **Approach:** Build in slack and devote resources to preparedness—for instance, stockpile inventory or overbuy talent. These steps are typically expensive; your investment should match the risk.

How well can you predict the results of your actions? (+)

complexity

Characteristics: The situation has many interconnected parts and variables. Some information is available or can be predicted, but the volume or nature of it can be overwhelming to process.

Example: You are doing business in many countries, all with unique regulatory environments, tariffs, and cultural values.

Approach: Restructure, bring on or develop specialists, and build up resources adequate to address the complexity.

volatility

Characteristics: The challenge is unexpected or unstable and may be of unknown duration, but it's not necessarily hard to understand; knowledge about it is often available.

Example: Prices fluctuate after a natural disaster takes a supplier off-line.

Approach: Build in slack and devote resources to preparedness—for instance, stockpile inventory or overbuy talent. These steps are typically expensive; your investment should match the risk.

ambiguity

Characteristics: Causal relationships are completely unclear. No precedents exist; you face "unknown unknowns."

Example: You decide to move into immature or emerging markets or to launch products outside your core competencies.

Approach: Experiment. Understanding cause and effect requires generating hypotheses and testing them. Design your experiments so that lessons learned can be broadly applied.

uncertainty

Characteristics: Despite a lack of other information, the event's basic cause and effect are known. Change is possible but not a given.

Example: A competitor's pending product launch muddies the future of the business and the market.

Approach: Invest in information—collect, interpret, and share it. This works best in conjunction with structural changes, such as adding information analysis networks, that can reduce ongoing uncertainty.

HOW MUCH DO YOU KNOW ABOUT THE SITUATION? (−) (+)

4. Uncertainty

- **Characteristics:** Despite a lack of other information, the event's basic cause and effect are known. Change is possible but not a given.
- **Example:** A competitor's pending product launch muddies the future of the business and the market.
- **Approach:** Invest in information—collect, interpret, and share it. This works best in conjunction with structural changes, such as adding information analysis networks, that can reduce ongoing uncertainty.

CHAPTER 3

Deciding How to Decide

A tool kit for executives making high-risk strategic bets by Hugh Courtney, Dan Lovallo, and Carmina Clarke

Senior managers are paid to make tough decisions. Much rides on the outcome of those decisions, and executives are judged—quite rightly—on their overall success rate. It's impossible to eliminate risk from strategic decision making, of course. But we believe that it is possible for executives—and companies—to significantly improve their chances of success by making one straightforward (albeit not simple) change: expanding their tool kit of decision support tools and understanding which tools work best for which decisions.

Most companies overrely on basic tools like discounted cash flow analysis or very simple quantitative scenario testing, even when they're facing highly complex, uncertain contexts. We see this constantly in our consulting and executive education work, and research bears out our impressions. Don't misunderstand. The conventional tools we all learned in business school are terrific when you're working in a stable environment, with a business model you understand and access to sound information. They're far less useful if you're on unfamiliar terrain—if you're in a fast-changing industry, launching a new kind of product, or shifting to a new business model. That's because conventional tools assume that decision makers have access to remarkably complete and reliable information. Yet every business leader we have worked with over the past 20 years acknowledges that more and more decisions involve judgments that must be made with incomplete and uncertain information.

The problem managers face is not a lack of appropriate tools. A wide variety of tools—including case-based decision analysis, qualitative scenario analysis, and information markets—can be used for decisions made under high degrees of uncertainty. But the sheer variety can be overwhelming without clear guidance about when to use one tool or combination of tools over another. Absent such guidance, decision makers will continue to rely solely on the tools they know best in an honest but misguided attempt to impose logic and structure on their make-or-break decisions.

In the first half of this article, we describe a model for matching the decision-making tool to the decision at hand, on the basis of three factors: how well you understand the variables that will determine success, how well you can predict the range of possible outcomes, and how centralized the relevant information is. We make a strong case for increased use of case-based decision analysis (which relies on multiple analogies) and qualitative scenario analysis under conditions of uncertainty.

Inevitably, the model we propose simplifies a very complicated reality in order to uncover some important truths. (That's what models do.) In the second half of the article, we explore some of the most common complications: Most executives underestimate the uncertainty they face; organizational protocols can hinder decision making; and managers have little understanding of when it's ideal to use several different tools to analyze a decision, or when it makes sense to delay a decision until they can frame it better.

Developing a Decision Profile

As you ponder which tools are appropriate for a given context, you need to ask yourself two fundamental questions:

Do I know what it will take to succeed? You need to know whether you have a causal model— that is, a strong understanding of what critical success factors and economic conditions, in what combination, will lead to a successful outcome. Companies that repeatedly make similar decisions often have strong causal models. Consider a retailer that has launched outlets for years in one country, or one that has made many small acquisitions of adjacent competitors.

One simple test of the strength of your causal model is whether you can specify with confidence a set of "if-then" statements about the decision. ("If our proposed new process technology lowers costs by X% and we are able to achieve Y% market share by passing those savings on to our customers, then we should invest in this technology.") You should also be able to specify a financial model into which you can plug different assumptions (such as how much the technology lowers costs and how much market share you are able to capture).

For the vast majority of strategic decisions, executives can't specify a clear causal model. Some managers have a reasonably good idea of the critical success factors that matter, but not a complete picture—this would generally be true of a company developing a new product, for example. Others don't even know how to frame the decision—for instance, a company being disrupted by a new technology wielded by a firm outside its industry.

ASK YOURSELF:

- Do you understand what combination of critical success factors will determine whether your decision leads to a successful outcome?

- Do you know what metrics need to be met to ensure success?

- Do you have a precise understanding of—almost a recipe for—how to achieve success?

Can I predict the range of possible outcomes? In choosing the right decision-support tools, you also need to know whether it's possible to predict an outcome, or a range of outcomes, that could result from the decision.

Sometimes it's possible to predict a single outcome with reasonable certainty, as when a company has made similar decisions many times before. More often, decision makers can identify a range of possible outcomes, both for specific success factors and for the decision as a whole. Often they can also predict the probability of those outcomes. However, under conditions of uncertainty, it's common for executives not to be able to specify the range of possible outcomes or their probability of occurring with any real precision (even in instances where they understand critical success factors and the model for success).

ASK YOURSELF:

- Can you define the range of outcomes that could result from your decision, both in the aggregate and for each critical success factor?

- Can you gauge the probability of each outcome?

Diagnosing Your Decision

When choosing a decision support tool for a major investment, executives need to answer three questions:

- *Do I know what it will take to succeed? (or, Do I have a full causal model?)*

- *Can I predict the range of possible outcomes?*

- *Do I need to aggregate information?*

The answers will point to the best decision-support tools.

Choosing the Right Tools: Five Contexts

As the section "Diagnosing Your Decision" suggests, the answers to the questions above will point you to the best decision-support tools. (For brief definitions of each, see "Decision Support Tools: A Glossary.") In some cases you'll need just one tool; in others

16

you'll need a combination. Many of these tools will be familiar. However, the tool we advocate using most, case-based decision analysis, is not yet widely used, partly because the more formal, rigorous versions of it are relatively new and partly because executives typically underestimate the degree of uncertainty they face.

To illustrate, let's look at five scenarios that executives at McDonald's might face. (These are oversimplified for the sake of clarity.)

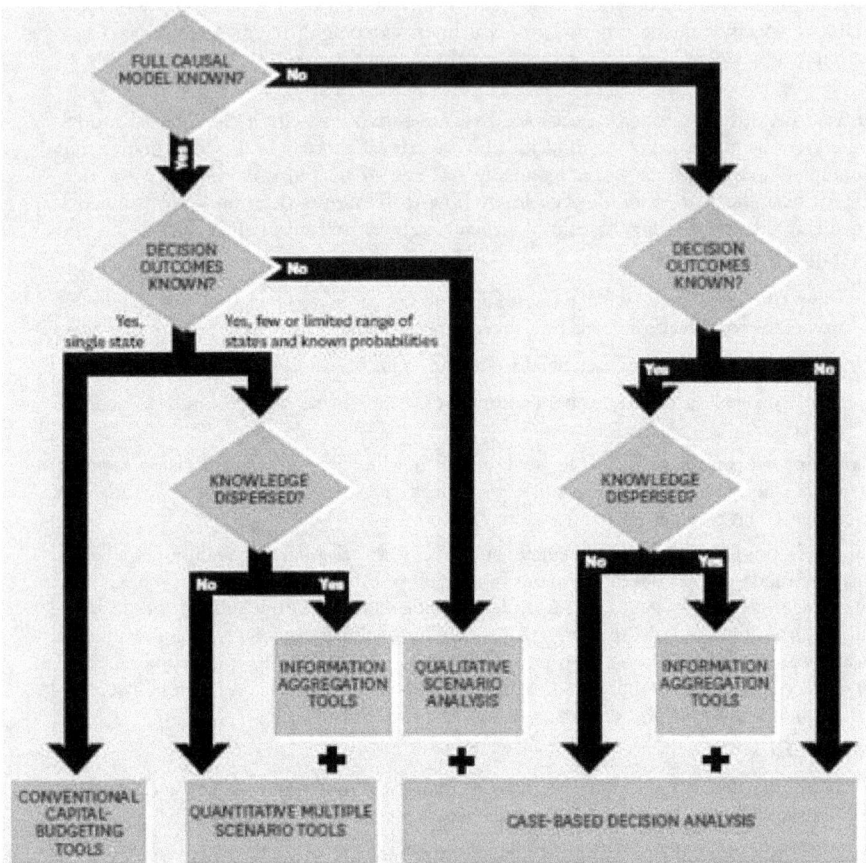

Situation 1: You understand your causal model and can predict the outcome of your decision with reasonable certainty. Suppose McDonald's executives must decide where to locate new U.S. restaurants. The company has or can get all the information it needs to be reasonably certain how a given location will perform. First, it knows the variables that matter for success: local demographics, traffic patterns, real estate availability and prices, and locations of competitive outlets. Second, it has or can obtain rich data sources on those variables. And third, it has well-calibrated restaurant revenue and cost models. Together that information constitutes a causal model. Decision makers can feed the information about traffic and other variables into standard discounted cash flow models to accurately predict (to a close-enough approximation) how the proposed location will perform and make a clear go/ no-go decision.

TOOLS: *Conventional capital-budgeting tools such as discounted cash flow and expected rate of return*

Situation 2: You understand your causal model and can predict a range of possible outcomes, along with probabilities for those outcomes. Imagine now that the McDonald's managers are deciding whether to introduce a new sandwich in the United States. They still have a reliable way to model costs and revenues; they have relevant data about demographics, foot traffic, and so forth. (In other words, they have a causal model.) But there's significant uncertainty about what the outcome of introducing the sandwich will be: They don't know what the demand will be, for example, nor do they know what impact the new product will have on sales of complementary products. However, they can predict a range of possible outcomes by using quantitative multiple scenario tools. Some preliminary market research in different regions of the country will most likely give them a range of outcomes, and perhaps even the probability of each. It might be possible to summarize this information in simple outcome trees that show the probability of different demand outcomes and the associated payoffs for McDonald's. The trees could be used to calculate the expected value, variance, and range of financial outcomes that McDonald's might face if it introduced the sandwich. Managers could then use standard decision-analysis techniques to make its final determination.

Alternatively, McDonald's could pilot the new sandwich in a limited number of regions. Such pilots provide useful information about the potential total market demand without incurring the risk of a full-scale rollout. Conducting a pilot is akin to investing in an "option" that provides information and gives you the right but not the obligation to roll out the product more extensively in the future. (This approach is still market research, but usually a more expensive form.) Real options analysis, which quantifies the benefits and costs of the pilot in light of market uncertainty, would be the appropriate decision-making tool in this case

TOOLS: *Quantitative multiple scenario tools such as Monte Carlo simulations, decision analysis, and real options valuation. (These tools combine statistical methods with the conventional capital-budgeting models favored in Situation 1. Managers can simulate possible outcomes using known probabilities and discounted cash flow models and then use decision analysis tools to calculate expected values, ranges, and so on.)*

Situation 3: You understand your causal model but cannot predict outcomes. Let's now assume that McDonald's is entering an emerging market for the first time. Executives still understand the model that will drive store profitability. The cost and revenue drivers may well be the same, market to market. However, the company has much less information about outcomes, and predicting them using market research and statistical analysis would be difficult. Its products are relatively novel in this market, it will be facing unfamiliar competitors, it's less sure of supplier reliability, and it knows less about whom to hire and how to train them. In this situation, McDonald's can use qualitative scenario analysis to get a better sense of possible outcomes. It can build scenarios on the revenue side that cover a wide range of customer acceptance and competitor response profiles. On the supply side, scenarios might focus on uncertainties in the emerging market supply chain and regulatory structure that could cause wide variation in supplier costs and reliability. These scenarios will be representative, not comprehensive, but they will help executives assess the upsides and downsides of various approaches and determine how much they are willing to invest in the market. Executives should supplement the scenarios with case-based decision analysis of analogous business situations. They might look at outcomes from their own or other fast-food entries in developing markets or consider outcomes from a consumer goods entry in this particular market.

TOOLS: *Qualitative scenario analysis supplemented with case-based decision analysis*

Situation 4: You don't understand your causal model, but you can still predict a range of outcomes. Suppose McDonald's wants to enter a new line of business with a new business model, such as consulting services for food-service process improvements. In this case, executives probably can't define a full causal model or easily identify the drivers of success. However, that doesn't mean they can't define a range of possible outcomes for the venture by tapping into the right information sources—for example, by getting estimates of success from people who have more experience with this business model or by aggregating information about the range of outcomes experienced by others using similar business models. It's often easier to tap into outcome data (and thus define a range of possible outcomes) that define an underlying business model than to ask people to reveal the details of their business models. (That "secret sauce" is confidential in many companies.)

TOOLS: *Case-based decision analysis*

Situation 5: You don't understand your causal model, and you can't predict a range of outcomes. Even a well-established market leader in a well-established industry faces decisions under high levels of ambiguity and uncertainty. When considering how to respond to the recent concern about obesity in the U.S. and the backlash over the fast-food industry's role in the obesity epidemic, McDonald's can't be sure of what effect various moves might have on customer demand. The backlash has the potential to fundamentally rewrite the rules for leadership in the fast-food industry and to make existing decision-making models and historical data obsolete. McDonald's certainly can't accurately forecast future lawsuits, medical research, legislative changes, and competitor moves that will ultimately determine the payoffs of any decisions it makes. When faced with this level of uncertainty, the company should once again rely on case-based decision analysis. Relevant reference cases might include other consumer goods companies' attempts to reposition themselves as healthy or safe alternatives in an otherwise "dangerous" sector or to influence legislation, regulation, or stakeholder perceptions through public relations and lobbying campaigns. McDonald's might analyze, for example, cases in the gaming, tobacco, firearms, carbonated beverage, and baked goods industries for insights.

TOOLS: *Case-based decision analysis*

Aggregating Information

Careful readers will have noticed that the decision tree has one set of tools we have not covered: information aggregation tools. We treat these separately because, for the most part, they function independently of the decision profile questions we pose at the top (do you have a causal model, and do you know the range of possible outcomes?).

The information that managers need in order to make strategic decisions is often dispersed and context-specific. For example, if a company is trying to gauge the synergies to be gained from a prospective acquisition, it's likely that different experts (inside and outside the firm) hold different pieces of relevant information. It's reasonably easy to gather the perspectives of these experts, using tools designed to aggregate information, and to generate a range of possible outcomes and their probabilities. Standard aggregation tools such as the Delphi approach have been in use for decades.

A newer approach to gathering dispersed information is to use information markets (also known as prediction markets) to capture the collective wisdom of informed crowds regarding key variables such as likely macroeconomic performance in the next year or how a proposed product will be received. We should note two limitations of this approach: First, because information and prediction markets are structured like financial securities markets, in which participants can "bet" on different outcomes, they can be used only when executives are able to specify a range of possible outcomes (as in situations 2 and 4 above). Second, using such markets may allow information to leak out that executives would prefer to keep private (for example, the expected revenue for a new drug).

Two alternatives to information markets can get around those limitations. The first is incentivized estimates: People who have access to diverse information are asked to provide estimates of a key outcome, and the person who comes closest to the actual number receives a payoff of some kind (which may or may not be monetary). The second is similarity-based forecasting: Individuals are asked to rate how similar a particular decision or asset is to past decisions or assets. The ratings are then aggregated using simple statistical procedures to generate forecasts for revenues or for completion times or costs, depending on the goal. (This is actually a case-based decision analysis tool.)

ASK YOURSELF:

- Is the information you need centralized or decentralized?
- If it's decentralized, can you tap the experts you need and aggregate their knowledge?
- Is it feasible and helpful to use "the crowd" for some portions of your information gathering?
- Is it possible to aggregate useful information from the crowd without having to reveal confidential information?

Complicating Factors

For the sake of clarity, we've presented a simplified set of examples above. In practice, of course, all kinds of complications occur when major decisions are being made. We explore a few of those below.

Executives don't know what they don't know. The model we've developed for choosing decision support tools is dependent on managers' being able to accurately determine the level of ambiguity and uncertainty they face. This may be problematic, because decision makers—like all human beings—are subject to cognitive limitations and behavioral biases. Particularly relevant here are the well-established facts that decision makers are overconfident of their ability to forecast uncertain outcomes and that they interpret data in ways that tend to confirm their initial hypotheses.

In essence, executives don't know what they don't know, but they're generally happy to assume that they do.

Cognitive bias creeps in. Managers' biased assessments of the level of uncertainty they face might lead some to conclude that our diagnostic tool is of limited practical use and might point them toward the wrong approach. Our consulting experiences suggest that most organizations can manage those biases if, when a strategic decision is being considered, managers choose their decision-making approach in a systematic, transparent, public manner during which their judgments can be evaluated by peers. (This will require process and culture change in many organizations.)

For example, any decision maker who assumes that she has a firm understanding of the economics underlying a big decision should be challenged with questions such as, Is there reason to believe that the relationship between critical success factors and outcomes has changed over time, making our historical models no longer valid? Similarly, those who assume that all possible outcomes and their probabilities can be identified ahead of time might be asked, Why are other seemingly plausible outcomes impossible? What assumptions are you making when estimating probabilities? Finally, those who conclude that the relevant information for making the decision resides within the company or even within a small group of senior executives might be asked, If we could put together a "dream team" to advise us on this decision, who would be on it and why?

When asked these questions, decision makers are less likely to assume that their decisions are straightforward or even intuitive and are more likely to turn to tools like scenario analysis and case-based decision making. This is especially important when a relatively new or unique strategic investment is under consideration.

Organizational processes get in the way. Organizations need to develop general protocols for decision making, because political and behavioral pitfalls are rife when money or power is at stake. Here's just one of many examples we could give: We worked with a leading technology company whose forecasting group used the same decision-support tool regardless of where a product was in its life cycle. This made no sense at all. When we investigated, we learned two things: First, business unit heads demanded simple forecasts because they didn't understand how to interpret or use complex ones. Second, the company did not charge business units for the capital used in R&D investments, so unit heads pushed the forecasting team to raise their revenue estimates. As a result of these factors, the forecasts were badly distorted. It would have made more sense for the forecasting team to report to the CFO, who was more sophisticated about financial modeling and also could be more objective about business units' investment needs. It's not possible to design all of the perverse incentives out of a system, but some commonsense protocols can make a big difference.

Decision makers tend to rely on a single tool. We were moved to create the decision profile diagnostic in part because we saw so many managers relying solely on conventional capital-budgeting techniques. Most important decisions involve degrees of ambiguity and uncertainty that those approaches aren't equipped to handle on their own.

It's often useful to supplement one tool with another or to combine tools. To illustrate this point, let's imagine that a Hollywood studio executive is charged with making a go/no-go decision about a mainstream movie. Decisions of this kind are vitally important: Today, the average production cost is $70 million for movies opening at 600 theaters or more (many have production budgets over $100 million), and only three or four out of every 10 movies break even or earn a profit. Yet the decision to green-light a project is usually based solely on "expert opinions"—in other words, executives' intuition supplemented by standard regression analysis. In a recent study, two of us used similarity-based forecasting to predict box office revenues for 19 wide-release movies. Nonexpert moviegoers were asked via online surveys to judge how similar each movie was—on the basis of a brief summary of the plot, stars, and other salient features—to other previously released movies. Revenues for the new movies were then forecasted by taking similarity-based weighted averages of the previously released movies' revenues. On average, those predictions were twice as accurate as ones driven by expert opinion and standard regression forecasting. They were particularly effective in identifying small revenue-earning movies. This type of case-based decision analysis is an effective way to tap into crowd wisdom.

Even in situations that seem relatively unambiguous, it often pays to supplement capital-budgeting and quantitative multiple scenario tools with case-based decision analyses to check for potential biases. For example, if your "certain" investment project is expected to deliver a rate of return that is unprecedented when compared with similar projects in the past, that might be more a reflection of overconfidence than of the extraordinary nature of your project. A robust analysis of analogous situations forces decision makers to look at their particular situation more objectively and tends to uncover any wishful thinking built into their return projections.

Managers don't consider the option to delay a decision. Deciding *when* to decide is often as important as deciding *how* to decide. In highly uncertain circumstances—such as a fast-changing industry or a major shift in business model—it's wise to borrow from a different tool kit altogether: learning-based, iterative experimentation. For instance, colleges today are being disrupted by massive open online courses (MOOCs), and most administrators don't know if or how or when their institutions should react. Rather than make an expensive, high-risk decision now, many colleges are undertaking small-scale experiments to test the waters and learn more about what "success" in this space will look like. (They're also using analogies, of course—for example, by trying to understand whether the unbundling of the music business has lessons for higher education.)

WHAT CAN you start doing tomorrow to become a better business decision maker? Begin by developing your decision-making tool kit more fully. There is a clear disconnect between the tools that are being used and those that should be used most often. Make it a priority to learn more about quantitative multiple scenario tools such as Monte Carlo simulations, decision analysis, and real options valuation. Get some training in scenario planning. Explore the fast-growing academic and practitioner literatures on information markets. Make more rigorous use of historical analogies to inform your most ambiguous and uncertain—and usually most important—decisions. We all use analogies, implicitly or explicitly, when making decisions. The cognitive scientist Douglas Hofstadter argues that analogy is the "fuel and fire of thinking." But it is far too easy to fall prey to our biases and focus on a limited set of self-serving analogies that support our preconceived notions. Those tendencies can be checked through rigorous case-based decision methods such as similarity-based forecasting.

Finally, and perhaps most important, make it a habit at your company to consciously decide how and when you are going to make any decision.

Decision Support Tools: A Glossary

CONVENTIONAL CAPITAL-BUDGETING TOOLS

These tools use the estimated incremental cash flows from potential investments to establish whether a project is worth being funded through the firm's capitalization structure. They include discounted cash flow, expected rate of return, and net present value models.

QUANTITATIVE MULTIPLE SCENARIO TOOLS

These tools analyze decisions by fully specifying possible outcomes and their probabilities. They use mathematical, statistical, and simulation methods to identify the risk/return properties of possible choices. The tools include:

- Monte Carlo methods, which use computational algorithms that rely on repeated random sampling to obtain numerical results
- decision analysis, which uses outcome scenarios and probabilities to identify the best decision to make given different decision-maker objectives
- real options, which applies the concept of financial option valuation to "real" situations and allows managers to quantify the costs and benefits of flexibility when making decisions under uncertainty

QUALITATIVE SCENARIO ANALYSIS

These tools inform decisions by developing a set of qualitative, representative scenarios of how the present may evolve into the future and identifying the likely consequences of the decision under consideration. Since these techniques don't assume a complete and fully specified set of possible outcomes, they are helpful to decision makers who face high levels of uncertainty about outcomes.

CASE-BASED DECISION ANALYSIS

These tools provide a systematic approach to aggregating and synthesizing information from analogous past experiences and examples. In general, analogies that are most similar to the decision at hand are given more weight in determining the best choice.

INFORMATION AGGREGATION TOOLS

These tools are used to collect information from diverse sources.

- Traditional approaches, including the Delphi method, gather information from a variety of expert sources, aggregate the responses, and generate a range of possible outcomes and their probabilities. Decision makers may then consult with the group again until a consensus is reached.
- Prediction or information markets are designed to gather "the wisdom of the crowd" by creating financial markets where investors can trade securities with payoffs linked to uncertain future outcomes (for example, the winner of an election or the release date of a new product).

- Incentivized estimate approaches involve surveying individuals with diverse information sources to estimate the outcomes of variables and then rewarding individuals with the most accurate estimates.

- Similarity-based forecasting methods involve asking individuals to rate how similar a decision or asset is to past decisions or assets. These similarity ratings are then aggregated across individuals using simple statistical procedures to generate forecasts (for revenues, completion times, or costs) depending on the goal. Since these methods rely on past decisions and outcomes, they are a form of case-based decision analysis as well.

Developing Rigorous Analogies: An Underutilized Tool

Although business leaders frequently use analogies to inform their decisions, many don't do so in a rigorous, systematic way.

For example, it is natural to fixate on the analogous situation that best supports the action you would like to take, ignoring other cases that might provide a broader picture of possible strategies and their outcomes. Case-based decision making provides a structured framework for synthesizing information from multiple analogous experiences and examples. Even when decision makers don't know the exact relationship between critical success factors and outcomes, they can use this method to learn from past successes and failures.

These methods require decision makers to collect a sample of analogous cases, determine the results achieved in those cases, and assess how similar each case is to the decision at hand. The best decision, then, is the one that maximizes the similarity-weighted average of results in the analogous cases. Sometimes the analogy is close to home: Movie producers can compare a project with similar projects from the past; serial acquirers can do the same. Decision makers on less familiar terrain must look to other industries for comparisons, and those comparisons will take more ingenuity. (Here it's essential to use structured frameworks for comparison.) Consumer product industries facing digital disruption might look to the unbundling of music and books as an analogy. A company shifting from a product-based to a service-based business model might look at IT companies that have made this shift. When decision makers can't build their own causal models of success, the best they can do is study the successes and failures of others in analogous situations, putting greater weight on the analogies that best fit their own situation.

The Idea in Brief

THE PROBLEM. In highly complex, uncertain contexts, traditional decision-support tools such as discounted cash flow analysis are worse than useless. Nonetheless, executives use them all the time.

THE SOLUTION. Good analytic tools exist for all strategic contexts. If you use the right tool, the odds of making a good decision go way up. Here, the authors present a model for matching the decision-making tool to the decision at hand, on the basis of three factors: how well you understand the variables that will determine success, how well you can predict the range of possible outcomes, and how centralized the relevant information is.

THE EXAMPLE. The authors illustrate their framework using decisions that executives at McDonald's might need to make—from very clear-cut (choosing a site for a new store in the United States) to highly uncertain (changing the business in response to the obesity epidemic).

CHAPTER 4

Stress-Test Your Strategy: The 7 Questions to Ask

An economic downturn can quickly expose the shortcomings of your business strategy. But can you identify its weak points in good times as well? And can you focus on those weak points that really matter?

A stress test—an assessment of how a system functions under severe or unexpected pressure—can help you home in on the most important issues to address, whatever the economic climate. By asking tough questions about your business, you can identify confusion, inefficiency, and weaknesses in your strategy and its implementation.

As Peter Drucker once warned, "The most serious mistakes are not being made as a result of wrong answers. The truly dangerous thing is asking the wrong questions." For the past 25 years I have researched the drivers of successful strategy execution in a variety of companies and industries. Through this work I have identified seven questions that all executives should ask—and be able to answer. Master this list, and you will keep the fundamentals of your strategy execution on track.

The questions may seem obvious, but the choices they represent can be tough, and their full implications are not always immediately clear. The first two questions compel you to set strict priorities. The next two assess your ability to focus on those priorities by designating critical performance variables and constraints. Questions five and six investigate whether you are using techniques that will enhance creative tension and commitment. The final question deals with your ability to adapt your strategy over time.

Let's take a look at each question, so that you can see how you—and your strategy—measure up.

The Seven Questions

1. Who is your primary customer?
2. How do your core values prioritize shareholders, employees, and customers?
3. What critical performance variables are you tracking?
4. What strategic boundaries have you set?
5. How are you generating creative tension?
6. How committed are your employees to helping each other?
7. What strategic uncertainties keep you awake at night?

1: Who Is Your Primary Customer?

Choosing a primary customer is a make-orbreak decision. Why? Because it should determine how you allocate resources. The idea is simple: Allocate all possible resources to meet and exceed your primary customer's needs.

Consider McDonald's, whose 32,000 restaurants feed more than 58 million customers each day. The company's growth over its 50-year history has been described as the greatest retail expansion in the history of the world.

What was the fast-food chain's key to success? A clear choice of a primary customer and an understanding of when that choice needed to change. In the 1980s and 1990s, McDonald's

24

considered its primary customers to be not the people who ate in its restaurants but multisite real estate developers and franchise owners. By focusing most of its resources on those customers through centralized real estate development, franchising, and procurement functions, it opened as many as 1,700 new stores a year.

But by 2003 same-store sales were declining. Worldwide markets were saturated, and people were tiring of the chain's standardized fare. This crisis prompted the new CEO at the time, Jim Cantalupo, to make a tough decision: "The new boss at McDonald's is the consumer," he announced.

The company's subsequent changes in resource allocation reveal the profound implications of this decision. Consumers' tastes differ widely by region and throughout the many countries in which McDonald's operates. To satisfy these varying tastes, McDonald's reallocated resources from centralized corporate functions to regional managers, who were encouraged to customize local menus and store amenities. In the United Kingdom, Mc-Donald's now serves porridge for breakfast; in Portugal, it offers soup; in France, it sells burgers topped with French cheese. The Paris design center provides franchisees with nine different design options, allowing them to customize the decor for their clientele.

As of last January, McDonald's had delivered 81 consecutive months of increasing samestore sales around the world. Its customer satisfaction scores rose each year from 2005 to 2009 (they faltered slightly in early 2010, as more upscale customers began to choose Mc-Donald's over pricier alternatives). It's no accident that McDonald's was one of only two companies in the Dow Jones Industrial Average to end 2008 with a gain in stock price.

Unlike McDonald's, many companies resist choosing just one customer. Executives often attempt to avoid the adjective "primary" by announcing, "We have multiple customers." This is a sure recipe for underperformance. Allocating resources to more than one customer results in confusion and less-than-optimal service.

Trying to accommodate multiple kinds of customers led to trouble at Home Depot. After taking over as CEO in 2000, Bob Nardelli concluded that the consumer home improvement business was saturated, and shifted significant resources away from consumers in order to cater to professional contractors. Consumers would no longer be the primary customers— but it wasn't clear that professional contractors were filling that role, either. Home Depot laid off customer service employees—the ones walking the aisles in orange aprons at its 1,900 stores—and spent the savings on an $8 billion acquisition spree, snapping up 30 wholesale housing-supply companies.

The acquisitions nearly doubled company revenue, but even so there weren't enough resources to meet the needs of two such different types of customers (there never are), and neither group was well served. During Nardelli's tenure Home Depot's consumer satisfaction scores suffered the biggest drop of any U.S. retailer ever. At the same time, the wholesale supply operation was not getting the support required to obtain the efficiencies needed for a low-margin business.

It took a new CEO, Frank Blake, to refocus the business. In 2007 he announced that home owners would again be the primary customers. Home Depot sold its wholesale businesses, increased the number of orange aprons on the floor, and rehired master trade specialists to offer consumers how-to advice. Consumer satisfaction scores and same-store sales and profits have begun to rebound.

Of course, your choice of primary customer may change over time—recall what happened at McDonald's. But you need to recognize that such a change will probably require restructuring your business.

The flip side of maximizing resources for your primary customer is that you should minimize the resources devoted to everything else including all external stakeholders and all internal units that do not create value for your primary customer. They should receive enough to meet the needs of their constituents, but no more.

2: How Do Your Core Values Prioritize Shareholders, Employees, and Customers?

Companies that execute strategy well define their core values to reflect the relative impor tance of shareholders, employees, and customers. Value statements that list aspirational behaviors aren't enough. *Core* values must indicate whose interests come first when difficult trade-offs must be made.

At some companies, customers come first. At others, it may be shareholders. At yet others, it may be employees. There is no right or wrong choice. Each choice is based on a different theory of value creation. But making one and communicating it effectively are essential.

A case in point is Merck's costly decision to withdraw Vioxx, its blockbuster Cox-2 pain suppressant, from the market. On September 24, 2004, then-CEO Ray Gilmartin got a call from the head of Merck's research labs, informing him that the preliminary results of an ongoing clinical study indicated that Vioxx caused unexpectedly high numbers of heart attacks and strokes after 18 months of continuous use. Gilmartin had three options: Merck could carry the study through to its planned conclusion to gather more data. It could ask the FDA to approve a "black box" label warning doctors and patients about the newly discovered risks. Or it could take the drug off the market, forgoing $2.5 billion in annual revenue.

On September 30—six days after the phone call—Gilmartin convened a press conference to announce the worldwide withdrawal of Vioxx. He explained his decision by citing the company's core value: "Merck puts patients first."

In contrast, Pfizer executives put shareholders first when faced with a similar situation. After discovering that Celebrex—the Cox-2 inhibitor Pfizer acquired when it bought Pharmacia— sometimes caused cardiovascular problems, they decided to keep manufacturing the drug. But they did so responsibly, adding a black box warning that allowed patients and doctors to make fully informed decisions. Shareholders thus avoided losing billions of dollars in profits.

A third option is to put employees first—a choice that can actually keep customers and shareholders content as well. As the former Southwest CEO Herb Kelleher has argued, "If employees are treated well, they'll treat the customers well. If the customers are treated well, they'll come back, and the shareholders will be happy." To drive this point home, Kelleher regularly appeared in national newspaper ads under the caption "Employees first. Customers second. Shareholders third." Other companies have made and communicated a similar choice.

Each of these rankings worked because the company made a clear decision and implemented it consistently. This is not always the case. Confusion about core values was at the root of the recent Fannie Mae debacle. Company executives, acting at politicians' behest, dedicated $1 trillion to democratizing home ownership by offering mortgages to disadvantaged customers. However, they were also trying to maximize shareholder value. To boost short-term profits, they built up and sold increasingly risky loan portfolios—until the housing market collapsed, leaving taxpayers with a $100 billion bailout bill.

3: What Critical Performance Variables Are You Tracking?

Many managers complain that they're overwhelmed by how many things they're asked to keep track of in all-inclusive lists of performance measures. It's not uncommon for companies to create scorecards with 30, 40, or more variables, in the mistaken belief that adding measures results in a more complete—and therefore better—scorecard. Information technology enables us to gather more and more data at lower and lower cost. But we cannot keep tracking so many variables. Effective managers monitor only a small number—those that could cause their strategy to fail.

The problems generated by trying to track too much data became evident at Citibank in the late 1990s, after executives introduced a new scorecard in their consumer bank. In addition to traditional financial measures, the card included new metrics for such things as strategy implementation and customer satisfaction.

As one district manager was pondering the award level for her top branch manager, conflicting signals from the new scorecard stopped her short. Although the branch manager had delivered outstanding financials, his customer satisfaction scores were subpar. The system would not permit a full bonus unless every measure was rated at par or above. Making an exception for one person could destroy the integrity of the system. But the branch manager might leave for a competitor if the scorecard undervalued his contribution. In the end his manager fudged the scorecard to ensure that he received an acceptable bonus. Because of similar problems involving other employees, the bank soon dropped the new scorecard.

Apart from avoiding this sort of dilemma, there is a simple but often overlooked reason to measure just a few variables: Management attention is your scarcest resource. As you add metrics to your scorecards, you incur an opportunity cost, in that people have less time to focus on what really matters. Think of Amazon, where inconvenience for buyers tops the list of factors that could cause strategy to fail. Executives there focus relentlessly on making purchasing as easy as possible: They concentrate on revenue per click and revenue per page turn, not on long lists of measures that have little to do with the customer's purchasing experience. At Nordstrom customer loyalty is key, so executives keep their attention on sales per hour and revenue per square foot. At Marriott the crucial metrics are associate satisfaction, guest satisfaction, revenue, and Rev- PAR (revenue per available room).

There's another reason to limit your focus: If you add too many measures to your scorecards, you will drive out innovation. In the old McDonald's—the one that prioritized franchise growth and standardized food—field consultants visited each store to measure its compliance with prescribed operating standards. They analyzed 500 metrics, producing a 25-page report on each store. With all the constraints imposed by these measures, store managers had no opportunity to innovate or respond to consumer preferences. Standardized mediocrity was the result.

4: What Strategic Boundaries Have You Set?

Every strategy carries the risk that an individual's actions will push the business off course. The risk intensifies when managers feel pressure to hit growth and profit targets.

There are two ways to control such risk: You can tell people what to do, or you can tell them what *not* to do. Telling people what to do helps assure that they won't make mistakes by engaging in unauthorized activities. This is the prudent approach if safety and quality are paramount concerns—if, say, you're running a nuclear power plant or overseeing a space launch. In such cases you want employees to follow standard operating procedures to the letter.

However, if innovation and entrepreneurial thinking are important, you should follow a different course: You should hire creative people and tell them what not to do. In other words, you should give them freedom to exercise their creativity—within defined limits.

Steve Jobs followed this principle when he declared that Apple would not develop a PDA. He later argued that without such discipline, the company wouldn't have had the resources to develop the iPod. "People think focus means saying yes to the thing you've got to focus on," he later said. "But that's not what it means at all. It means saying no to the hundred other good ideas."

Setting clear boundaries also lets organizations avoid the waste and risk that inevitably accompany undisciplined growth. To take one dramatic example, Wells Fargo weathered the 2008–2009 financial crisis because it strictly forbade its employees to venture into structured investment products and low-documentation mortgage loans. Unlike most of its competitors, Wells Fargo also refused to court future business from Warren Buffett by lending money to Berkshire Hathaway at belowmarket rates. This decision actually won Buffett's respect. "I got a big kick out of that, because that was exactly how they should think," he told *Fortune*. "The real insight you get about a banker is...what they don't do. And what Wells didn't do is what defines their greatness."

But remember: Boundaries are powered by punishment, not rewards. You must be willing to discipline—and fire, if necessary—anyone caught stepping over the line. If you follow up forcefully and consistently, word will travel throughout your organization, reinforcing the importance of your prohibitions.

5: How Are You Generating Creative Tension?

As a business leader, one of your primary jobs is to make outside market pressures felt inside your business. This can motivate employees to think and act like winning competitors, rousing them from comfortable ruts. The bigger your business, the more insulated people are from market pressures, and the more imperative this becomes.

Here is a menu of techniques that can generate creative tension and spur innovation. In this instance, unlike when defining a primary customer or ranking your responsibilities, you needn't choose just one; choose whichever and however many are right for your company. In fact, the more innovation you desire, the more techniques you should consider.

Assigning stretch goals. The most common way of motivating people to innovate is to set stretch goals—sometimes called challenge goals or big, hairy, audacious goals. Conducting business as usual or making incremental improvements is not enough. The only way to meet aggressive targets is to do something completely different.

Ranking according to performance. Many high-innovation organizations rank employees on the basis of demonstrated performance. The rankings affect who is promoted, who is placed on probation, and who is asked to leave. The challenge, of course, is to prevent the competition from becoming negative and destructive.

GE's Jack Welch is unapologetic when he argues the merits of this approach. The ranking system at GE was "very controversial," he has said. "Weed out the weakest....It's been portrayed as a cruel system. It isn't. The cruel system is the one that doesn't tell anybody where they stand."

You can take this approach a step further by ranking the performance of teams and business units. This will unquestionably produce adrenaline to compete and to innovate. Nike's CEO, Mark Parker, likes to fire up friendly rivalries by posting each footwear division's performance scores after every season. "People see each other's scores, and they huddle and really look at how they can make it better next season," he has explained.

Setting spans of accountability that are greater than spans of control.

If you want people to innovate, try holding them accountable for measures that are broader than the resources they control. This is the well-worn path followed by every successful entrepreneur, and you can use it to foster entrepreneurial behavior within your business.

Tom Siebel, of Siebel Systems, understood this principle well when he based his managers' bonuses on customer satisfaction measures, even though no one manager controlled all the resources needed to make a customer happy. His action forced the managers to innovate their way to success. As one business unit head put it, "To do my day-to-day job, I depend on sales, sales consulting, competency groups, alliances, technical support, corporate marketing, field marketing, and integrated marketing communications. None of these functions report to me....Coordination happens because we all have customer satisfaction as our first priority."

Allocating costs. The way in which you charge corporate overhead costs can also stimulate creative tension. Jamie Dimon, the CEO of JPMorgan Chase, insists on full allocation of overhead—everything from legal to marketing expenses—to the parts of the business that use them.

The purpose here is twofold. The most obvious goal is to generate accurate cost data. But often the more important one is to motivate managers to become actively involved in discussions about the value of corporate services provided. When operating managers have skin in the game, they will generate ideas about how units can work together to do things better, faster, or cheaper.

Creating cross-unit teams and matrix accountability. Another way of forcing employees to think outside the box is to assign them to a second box. New perspectives emerge when people are forced out of their routines. When they attend cross-unit team meetings, employees not only serve as emissaries for their home units but also return with ideas and innovations from their new colleagues.

You can push this approach to an extreme by adopting a matrix design, in which every manager has two bosses. One may be a regional head, the other a product market head. Everyone in the matrix is then accountable for conflicting priorities. Many global companies, including ABB, Novartis, and P&G, have at one time or another used this approach.

As with each of these techniques, you must be careful to balance the benefits and costs. On one hand, you will generate creative tension as people present and negotiate multiple points of view. On the other hand, you risk having the added bureaucracy slow down decision making. When P&G adopted a matrix structure, global product leaders had to get approval from the relevant regional head whenever they wanted to introduce a new product. Too many people had veto power. So in 2005 P&G abandoned the matrix in favor of global business units.

6: How Committed Are Your Employees to Helping Each Other?

Although you want your employees to achieve their personal best, they must also work to gether toward shared goals. To create the high levels of commitment that requires, leaders must build an organization that has the following four attributes:

Pride in purpose. If people are proud of their organization's mission, they will assume shared responsibility for its success. The sort of pride embodied in the Marine Corps slogan "Semper fidelis" ("Always faithful") is echoed in Merck's "Putting patients first" and Amazon's "Earth's most customer-centric company." In each case the tagline inspires and motivates members of the organization.

Group identification. Belonging to an elite organization is itself a source of pride, one that carries with it a sense of responsibility toward others in the group. In the Marines ("The few. The proud"), the first loyalty of every member is to the unit—to helping those in it no matter what.

The same principle can apply to businesses. Employees of Southwest Airlines, for example, take pride in a rigorous selection process that admits fewer than 2% of the 100,000 annual applicants. To reinforce their identification with the company, employees from different departments are encouraged to interview job candidates and veto those they feel would not be a good fit. Applicants who are hired know they are part of an elite team whose members go above and beyond to help one another.

Trust. When you trust your colleagues, you're willing to make yourself vulnerable—to put your reputation on the line to support them. Trust is vital if you want people to work collaboratively. At Nucor, the industry-leading steel company, employees are encouraged to propose innovations to improve efficiency. Nucor shares the resulting savings with its employees, rather than increasing production targets. This policy has built trust among the workers, who are confident that they and the executives are working together toward the same goals.

Fairness. The final requirement for collaboration is fairness. Disparities in compensation among peers pose the most obvious challenge: Nothing is more certain to kill the desire to help a colleague. In themselves, inequities in pay are easy to fix; far more insidious are perks signaling that those at the top are more deserving than everyone else. To guard against this danger, Southwest's highest executives work out of small interior offices that have been described as only slightly nicer than janitors' closets.

Vertical pay inequity is also an issue; if you want people to commit to helping one another, you must share rewards fairly up and down the organization. Southwest has operated with a rule that executive pay increases cannot be larger, proportionately, than other employees' raises. And in bad times executives take pay reductions along with everyone else. An industry analyst once calculated that as a result of these practices, Southwest generated 10 times more revenue for every dollar of executive compensation than some of its big U.S. competitors.

If you want your employees to embrace your vision of shared success, you must be perceived as putting fairness and equity above self-interest. When Sam Palmisano took over as IBM's CEO, he asked the board to reallocate half of his bonus to the executives who would be leading his new, team-based strategy. And early last year, when he announced that 250,000 IBM employees would be getting raises, he added, "The executives won't—but that's fine. We make enough money!"

7: What Strategic Uncertainties Keep You Awake at Night?

At the root of every failed strategy is a set of assumptions about the future that eventually proved false. We assumed housing prices would never fall simultaneously across the country. We assumed asset diversification would eliminate risk. We assumed the migration to digital media would be slow and orderly. We assumed customers wouldn't accept fewer features in exchange for a lower price.

Only three things in life are certain: death, taxes, and the fact that today's strategy won't work tomorrow. At some point your products will become obsolete, your customers' tastes will change, or technology will render your business model uncompetitive. Today's successes will be tomorrow's old news. The question is not if, but when.

To adapt successfully, you must constantly monitor the uncertainties that could invalidate the assumptions underpinning your current strategy. Your entire organization must continually scan the competitive environment for changes and send intelligence up the line. And because everyone watches what the boss watches, if you want your employees to focus on specific issues, focus on those issues yourself.

The most powerful way to signal what's important to you is to use your business control systems as interactive tools. Pay close—and visible—attention to the data they produce, and use them to generate questions that will activate the search for information throughout your business.

By using its P&L system interactively, Goldman Sachs avoided the mortgage-backed securities debacle that brought most of its competitors to their knees. A Goldman executive has described the process this way: "We look at the P&L of our businesses every day. We have lots of models that are important, but none are more important than the P&L, and we check every day to make sure our P&L is consistent with where our risk models say it should be. In December [of 2006] our mortgage business lost money for 10 days in a row. It wasn't a lot of money, but by the 10th day we thought that we should sit down and talk about it." The talk quickly turned into action: Goldman issued an order to reduce exposure to mortgage-backed securities and hedge remaining positions against future losses. This early move allowed the firm to prosper as competitors were forced to liquidate.

Depending on your business, the system you choose to use interactively could be a profit plan, a new-business booking system, or a project management system. Any performance measurement system will do as long as it contains easy-to-understand information, requires face-to-face interaction among operating managers, focuses dialogues on strategic uncertainties, and generates new action plans.

Once you've chosen a system, you must not only ask your employees to challenge deeply held assumptions, including your own, but also reward those who have the courage to tell you bad news. When Alan Mulally arrived at Ford as the CEO, he discovered that executives were afraid of admitting failure. Their presentations at Thursday morning meetings highlighted only successes (color-coded green), never problems (color-coded yellow and red). Mulally asked how everything could be so rosy when the company was losing billions. Mark Fields, the head of the Americas division, finally gave a presentation noting technical problems with the new Ford Edge. Everyone waited to see how the new boss would react. "The whole place was deathly silent," Mulally recalled in an interview with *Fortune*. "Then I clapped, and I said, 'Mark, I really appreciate that clear visibility.' And the next week the entire set of charts were all rainbows."

A Checklist for Executing Strategy

Executing strategy successfully requires making tough, often uncomfortable choices based on simple logic and clear principles. But we frequently avoid making choices, in the mistaken belief that we can have it all. Instead of focusing on one primary customer, we have many kinds of customers. Instead of instilling core values, we develop lists of desired behaviors. Instead of focusing on a few critical measures, we build overloaded scorecards.

There is no magic bullet that can zero in on the pitfalls of your business strategy. There is only one route to success: You must engage in ongoing, face-to-face debate with the people around you about emerging data, unspoken assumptions, difficult choices, and, ultimately, action plans. You and they should be able to give clear, consistent answers to the seven questions posed above. Only then can you be confident that your strategy is on track.

Ask the Whole Team

The seven questions are intended to be tools for stimulating engagement. Everyone in your business, from the CEO to the front line, must be actively involved in discussions about the key factors that will enable the successful execution of your strategy. Therefore, *how* you ask the questions is crucial. These commonsense principles will help you involve your whole team.

You must pose the questions face-toface.

"Look me in the eye" interaction is essential. You cannot get real engagement remotely or by e-mail. You must be able to see the subtle body language that can tell you when to challenge, probe, and push and when to offer encouragement and support.

Discussions must cascade down the organization, not stay stuck at the top.

The tone you set will echo throughout the business.

Your operating managers are key to the process.

Staff groups can play a useful role in data input, facilitation, and followup, but operating managers are the ones who can commit to action and who are responsible for results.

The debate must be about what is right, not who is right.

People should check titles and office politics at the door. You should encourage everyone to take risks, state unpopular opinions, and challenge the status quo.

You must root every discussion in the challenge "What are you going to do about it?"

Think of the seven questions as a means to an end. Their purpose is to inspire decisions and, ultimately, action.

The Idea in Brief

How do you identify the weakest parts of your strategy? Asking tough questions about your business—seven key questions in particular—will help you understand where confusion and inefficiency lie.

Have you identified a primary customer? Who is first among your stakeholders—shareholders, employees, or customers? Have you narrowed down which performance variables you track? Set critical boundaries? Do you generate creative tension? Promote coordination among your employees? And finally, what questions keep you up at night, thinking about how the future will change your business?

CHAPTER 5

Learning to Live With Complexity

How to make sense of the unpredictable and the undefinable in today's hyperconnected business world by Gökçe Sargut and Rita Gunther McGrath

Managing a business today is fundamentally different than it was just 30 years ago. The most profound difference, we've come to believe, is the level of complexity people have to cope with.

Complex systems have always existed, of course—and business life has always featured the unpredictable, the surprising, and the unexpected. But complexity has gone from something found mainly in large systems, such as cities, to something that affects almost everything we touch: the products we design, the jobs we do every day, and the organizations we oversee. Most of this increase has resulted from the information technology revolution of the past few decades. Systems that used to be separate are now interconnected and interdependent, which means that they are, by definition, more complex.

Complex organizations are far more difficult to manage than merely complicated ones. It's harder to predict what will happen, because complex systems interact in unexpected ways. It's harder to make sense of things, because the degree of complexity may lie beyond our cognitive limits. And it's harder to place bets, because the past behavior of a complex system may not predict its future behavior. In a complex system the outlier is often more significant than the average.

Making matters worse, our analytic tools haven't kept up. Collectively we know a good deal about how to navigate complexity—but that knowledge hasn't permeated the thinking of most of today's executives or the business schools that teach tomorrow's managers. How can we bring that knowledge to the fore?

Let's take a close look at what complexity is, the problems it raises, and how those problems can be addressed.

Complicated Versus Complex

It's easy to confuse the merely complicated with the genuinely complex. Managers need to know the difference: If you manage a complex organization as if it were just a complicated one, you'll make serious, expensive mistakes.

Let's back up and start with simple systems. These contain few interactions and are extremely predictable. Think of switching a light on and off: The same action produces the same result every time.

Complicated systems have many moving parts, but they operate in patterned ways. The electrical grid that powers the light is complicated: There are many possible interactions within it, but they usually follow a pattern. It's possible to make accurate predictions about how a complicated system will behave. For instance, flying a commercial airplane involves complicated but predictable steps, and as a result it's astonishingly safe. Implementing a Six Sigma process can be complicated, but the inputs, practices, and outputs are relatively easy to predict.

Complex systems, by contrast, are imbued with features that may operate in patterned ways but whose interactions are continually changing. Three properties determine the complexity of an environment. The first, *multiplicity*, refers to the number of potentially interacting elements. The second, *interdependence*, relates to how connected those elements are. The third, *diversity,* has to do with the degree of their heterogeneity. The greater the multiplicity, interdependence, and diversity, the greater the complexity. An organic growth program, for example, is highly complex—it contains a large number of interactive, interdependent, diverse elements.

Practically speaking, the main difference between complicated and complex systems is that with the former, one can usually predict outcomes by knowing the starting conditions. In a complex system, the same starting conditions can produce different outcomes, depending on the interactions of the elements in the system. Air traffic control, a complex system, constantly changes in reaction to weather, aircraft downtime, and so on. The system is predictable not because it produces the same results from the same starting conditions but because it has been designed to continuously adjust as its components change in relation to one another.

It's possible to understand both simple and complicated systems by identifying and modeling the relationships between the parts; the relationships can be reduced to clear, predictable interactions. It's not possible to understand complex systems in this way, because all the elements are interacting continuously and unpredictably.

The Problems of Complexity

We've observed two problems commonly faced by managers of complex systems: unintended consequences and difficulty making sense of a situation.

Unintended consequences. In a complex environment, even small decisions can have surprising effects. Researchers have identified three situations in which this is likely to happen. The first is when *events interact without anyone meaning them to.* Nintendo's Wii provides a recent example. Its innovative motion-sensing feature was designed to significantly expand the gaming market. To appeal to novice gamers and keep the price down, the company made the rest of the console relatively simple. It believed that its core audience would appreciate the new technology and forgive the less-sophisticated console. Nintendo succeeded in its immediate goal of pulling in new customers. But traditional, hard-core gamers saw the motion-sensing technology as a gimmick and perceived the system as unserious. Over time, third-party developers increasingly released titles for Xbox 360 and PlayStation 3 but not for the Wii—partly because of the console's limitations but also because they, too, had come to view the Wii as a "casual" gaming machine. This long-term consequence of the company's decisions would have been hard to foresee.

A positive unintended consequence occurred when Ford CEO Alan Mulally agreed to join his fellow U.S. automotive CEOs in testifying to Congress in support of an industry bailout—even though Ford was the only carmaker *not* requesting TARP money. (He did this in part because the industry's supply chains were so intertwined that a GM or Chrysler shutdown would have hurt Ford, too.) Press reports of his action were quite favorable, and public perception of Ford's quality and desirability rose dramatically.

The second situation concerns unintended consequences that are based on *an aggregate of individual elements,* not a single occurrence. The 2008 financial meltdown, for example, can be traced to numerous distinct but interconnected events: the relaxation of banking regulations, the invention of instruments that allowed lenders to shift risk off their balance sheets, monetary policies that kept interest rates low, the evaporation of reasonable credit standards and conventional down-payment requirements, ignorance on the part of borrowers, and so on. As we have now painfully learned, many observers could see some of these elements, but almost no one saw them all or anticipated the consequences of a drop in housing prices on the entire economic system.

A third situation is when *policies and procedures remain in place long after the reason for their creation becomes obsolete.* By then the logic underlying the procedures has often been forgotten. Employees at a major New York financial institution, for example, had to key in a code to enter the restrooms because of concerns about uninvited people gaining access. After 9/11 the firm instituted security screening at the building's entrance, making the restroom key codes unnecessary—but it took years to get rid of them! In the meantime, life was more difficult for employees, clients, suppliers, and other visitors, for no reason at all.

Making sense of a situation. It is very difficult, if not impossible, for an individual decision maker to see an entire complex system. This is essentially a *vantage point* problem: It's hard to observe and comprehend a highly diverse array of relationships from any one location. Many have argued that Citigroup's near collapse, in 2008, stemmed from an organizational design that locked people into silos; employees with information about the consequences of the bank's involvement in subprime lending were not connected to those making strategic decisions. It didn't help, of course, that the CEO at the time, Chuck Prince, conspicuously chose to ignore any warning signs of excessive leverage, as a now-famous remark to the *Financial Times* in 2007 demonstrates. "As long as the music is playing, you've got to get up and dance," Prince said, adding, "We're still dancing."

We are further hampered by *cognitive limits* to our understanding of the effects of other people's actions and our own. Most executives believe theycan take in and make sense of more information than research suggests they actually can. As a result, they often act prematurely, making major decisions without fully comprehending the likely consequences for the system. Durk Jager, the former head of Procter & Gamble, was pilloried for implementing sweeping organizational changes that mangled essential informal ties; in effect, he failed to grasp critical interdependencies in the firm. He lasted just 17 months in the top job. His successor, A.G. Lafley, did very little to change formal structures, focusing instead on realigning incentives and rebuilding informal connections. In June 2000, when Lafley took over, P&G's market capitalization was $69.8 billion. By 2007 it was $231.9 billion.

In addition, we now know that *focusing on one thing can prevent us from seeing others*. A recent study documented substantial "inattentional blindness": Subjects who had been instructed to concentrate on a task failed even to notice dramatic events going on around them.

Rare events pose particular problems for those trying to make sense of complex systems, because they don't repeat themselves often enough for us to learn how they will affect the system. Recall that air traffic control is generally a manageable system because it continuously adapts to changes. That adaptability is possible only because the system's designers (sense makers) observed patterns that emerged over time and found the root causes of failures by conducting excruciatingly thorough postmortem reviews. When the system was confronted with a rare event—the 2010 eruptions of Iceland's Eyjafjallajökull volcano, which created a dust cloud whose size and properties had never been encountered in aviation history—it could not cope and had to be shut down, at enormous expense. Similar systemic shutdowns followed Hurricane Katrina, in New Orleans, and the earthquake and tsunami in Japan.

Collectively, these problems mean that complex systems pose challenges in at least three areas of managerial activity: forecasting the future, mitigating risks, and making tradeoffs. Let's explore some remedies for each.

Improved Forecasting Methods

Managers faced with complex systems can take several steps to increase their predictive abilities. They should:

Drop certain forecasting tools. Embedded in many analytic tools are two assumptions that don't hold for complex systems. The first is that observations of phenomena are truly independent; this is often not the case in complex systems, with their highly interconnected parts. (Think of the wellknown "butterfly effect," when something small that happens early in a chain of events causes disproportionate consequences by the end.) The second is that it's possible to extrapolate averages or medians to entire populations. Take a controversial case in medicine—the U.S. Food and Drug Administration's deliberations (ongoing as of this writing) over whether to withdraw approval for the use of the drug Avastin in treating breast cancer. The issue has caused an uproar among the estimated 17,000 U.S. women who take the medication. Follow-up clinical trials revealed some potentially serious side effects and failed to show that the drug helps the statistically average patient. However, many doctors and patients have suggested that it prolongs life and improves quality of life in certain patients and completely cures a few. Cancer treatment is a complex system, but the agency is applying the logic of a complicated one.

In business, the problem shows up when companies try to predict customer behavior on the basis of average responses. On average, people loved New Coke, but the product ultimately flopped. It shows up when they fail to consider that outliers are often more interesting than the average case. And it shows up when they fail to account for the future importance of early events. Boston Scientific paid a huge amount for the cardiovascular device manufacturer Guidant, despite revelations during the bidding process of quality problems and cover-ups. Had it understood that those revelations signaled deeper problems going back many years, it could have avoided overpaying for a company it then had to pour vast resources into fixing. Boston Scientific's stock has yet to recover.

And in complex systems, events far from the median may be more common than we think. Tools that assume outliers to be rare can obscure the wide variations contained in complex systems. In the U.S. stock market, the 10 biggest one-day moves accounted for *half* the market returns over the past 50 years. Only a handful of analysts entertained the possibility of so many significant spikes when they constructed their predictive models.

Simulate the behavior of a system. Instead of extrapolating from irrelevant medians, look for modeling that will give you insight into the system and the ways in which its various elements interact. Examples include the customer-relationshipmanagement models used by telecommunications companies to anticipate a person's vulnerability to defection, and the data-mining tools used to predict consumer responses to various types of advertising. Further, make sure that your forecasting models incorporate low-probability but high-impact extremes. The complexity researchers Pierpaolo Andriani and Bill McKelvey observed that 16,000 minor earthquakes occur in California every year, but a really big one happens only once every 150 or 200 years. The average earthquake, then, is not very dangerous. It would be foolhardy, though, to base building codes on the average quake when what matters most is the big one. So, too, in business: What matters most may be the extreme but rare possibility, not the most likely one.

Use three types of predictive information. If it's impossible to predict the future in a complex system with a high degree of accuracy, and if organizations must nonetheless place bets with the future in mind, what's the wisest course for leaders who need to put some stakes in the ground? How can they find a happy medium between excessive and convoluted scenarios about what *might* happen and linear predictions that are over-reliant on past knowledge? We advise managers to be explicit about what they think will be applicable from past experience and what might be different this time around. One way to do this is to divide your data among three buckets:

Most financial metrics and key performance indicators fall into this bucket.

- Current: data about where you stand right now. Your pipeline of opportunities might be in this bucket.
- Leading: data about where things could go and how the system might respond to a range of possibilities.

If the bulk of your information is in the lagging bucket, that's a warning sign. Basing decisions mainly on lagging indicators is essentially betting that the future will be like the past. At least some of your information should be in the leading bucket. This information will be fuzzy and subjective by definition: The future hasn't happened yet. But without it, you're apt to be blindsided by change.

For an example of how the leading bucket prompted action to avert a possible system failure, recall the Y2K dilemma—the concern that computers would go haywire at the turn of the century because many used a two-digit year format. Early programmers expected that the software they created would be completely overhauled long before the millennium rolled over, but many critical legacy systems using the two-digit format remained (a fact we would place in the lagging bucket). The catastrophic scenarios in the leading bucket were so vivid and plausible that enormous efforts were made to bring complex computer systems into compliance before the year 2000 arrived (the plans to this end would be placed in the current bucket). When the time came, only a handful of problems surfaced, most of them minor.

Note that while the bucket tool simplifies reality, it doesn't assume away complexity, unlike traditional forecasting tools.

Better Risk Mitigation

Minimizing risk is crucial for anyone in charge of a complex system, and traditional approaches aren't good enough. Managers must learn to:

Limit or even eliminate the need for accurate predictions. In an unpredictable world, sometimes the best investments are those that minimize the importance of predictions. Take product design. In a conventional system, manufacturers must guess which configuration of features customers will purchase, and at what price. They run a high risk of being wrong, especially when the product is complex.

It's possible to eliminate this guesswork by designing a system that puts users in charge of the decisions, allowing them to create the outputs they want. Lulu, for example, has upended the traditional publishing model by giving writers control over key elements of the process. In the conventional model, publishers pay authors an advance and print books without knowing how many copies will sell. In the Lulu model, authors upload content to the company's website and name their price. The books (or other outputs) are printed only after customers visit the site and decide to buy them. The authors receive 80% of the revenue— more per copy than is typical—and Lulu avoids the risk of printing books that end up on the remainder table or in warehouses, or being destroyed. By structuring the decision process so that books are produced and funds change hands only when a buyer is ready to pay, Lulu has more or less eliminated the danger of getting it wrong.

Boeing's wildly successful 777 aircraft series exemplifies this principle at a much higher level of product complexity. The company engaged eight major airlines to help with the development process, producing iterative models whose design evolved according to these customers' input. It used advanced visualization techniques such as 3-D modeling to reduce unexpected interactions between airplane systems and capture feedback as early as possible.

Use decoupling and redundancy. Sometimes elements of a complex system can be separated from one another to decrease the systemic consequences if something goes wrong. Decoupling yields two benefits: It shields parts of the organization from the risks of an unexpected event, and it preserves parts that may be needed to mount a response. Contrast the Windows operating system with Software as a Service (SaaS) applications. With Windows, the operating system and your data are tightly entwined; when you upgrade to a new version of the system, all your information is erased, meaning that you need to back it up and reload it to your computer. With SaaS, uniform interfaces tell the computer where your data are. You can upgrade away, and the data won't be touched. And because the software and the data are uncoupled, the risk that both will be harmed simultaneously is significantly reduced.

Elements can also be designed to substitute for one another in case part of the system goes down. Intentional redundancy makes it more likely that the system can continue to operate to at least some degree even when portions of it are challenged. Decoupling and redundancy involve added expense, but the investment can be worthwhile.

Of course, there are limits to the decoupling and redundancy you can contain (and afford) within a single organization. You may need to call on external resources to expand the adaptive responses your organization can muster. The consultancy Accenture, for example, has an extensive network of partners to whom it can quickly turn if a client has an unanticipated need that Accenture cannot address. It also uses partnerships (including an arrangement with one of us, Rita) to conduct research that might not be part of its mainstream business but could yield early warnings of interest to its clients.

Draw on storytelling and counterfactuals. Another aspect of mitigating risk is making sure that people view unlikely but potentially catastrophic future events as real. Sharing anecdotes about near misses and rehearsing responses to a hypothesized negative event can help focus attention on a possibly significant future occurrence. Posing counterfactuals—asking "What if?"—is a terrific but surprisingly underutilized way of coming up with scenarios that are unlikely to be surfaced by traditional techniques. In business, "soft" approaches like these are valued less than the supposedly more rigorous activity of number crunching. We instinctively associate stories and counterfactuals with literature and fantasy and look to data for science, reason, and truth. But when traditional methods repeatedly fail to make sense of the rare and unexpected (precisely the things that most interest us), it's time to reconsider. Stories can give us great insights into complex systems, partly because the storyteller's reflections are not restricted by the available data.

Triangulate. As powerful as storytelling is, it comes with a disadvantage. The sky's the limit as far as our imagination goes—and therein lies the problem. There are no boundaries around where we should look or when we should stop looking. That's where triangulation comes into play.

Triangulation means attacking a problem from various angles—using different methodologies, making different assumptions, collecting different data, or looking at the same data in different ways. One of the best ways to understand a complex system is to do precisely that. For example, comparing snapshots of various elements taken at a given point in time (an activity social scientists call crosssectional analysis) yields a different understanding than looking at how a single element evolves over time. Or you can do both, studying how numerous elements evolve over time; in fact, this is the bread and butter of much sophisticated econometric and financial analysis. Despite its obvious advantages, triangulation had limited application until very recently, but the tools it requires have gotten better and easier to use.

Combining "soft" but flexible storytelling techniques with "hard" but rigid quantitative analyses can be an extremely powerful way to make sense of complex systems. The former help us explore unlikely but important possibilities and unintended consequences, while the latter give us concrete insights into the relationships of the system's visible components. Managers confronted with complexity should avail themselves of both.

Smart Tradeoff Decisions

In a complicated environment, it's relatively easy to make good tradeoffs: Simply figure out the optimal combination of elements and invest in those. It's similar to an engineering problem. In complex environments, however, making good tradeoffs is more difficult. Two strategies can help.

Take a real-options approach. This means making relatively small investments that give you the right, but not the obligation, to make further investments later on. The goal is to limit your downside while maximizing the value you can capture on the upside. Gradually building a portfolio of small investments keeps the stakes low until you're able to reduce the most significant uncertainties you face. A real-options strategy helps you manage failure by containing costs, not by eliminating risks (an approach Duke University's Sim Sitkin and others have called "intelligent failure"). The idea isn't to avoid making mistakes but to make them cheaply and early, learning from them and increasing your resilience as you go.

Ensure diversity of thought. What kinds of HR tradeoffs might you make if you realized you were dealing with a complex system rather than a merely complicated one? Complicated systems are like machines; above all, you need to minimize friction. Complex systems are organic; you need to make sure your organization contains enough diverse thinkers to deal with the changes and variations that will inevitably occur. Who in your company regularly talks to people you might not interact with yourself, comes up with things that are a little off the beaten track, and is attuned to underlying risks and trends that your other managers might overlook? In a complex system, finding the right people for the job means seeking out these sorts of thinkers (see the section "A Counterintuitive Approach to Hiring" for an unusual but effective strategy).

We have made tremendous progress in our ability to operate complicated systems, even large ones; we've done this by studying breakdowns and adjusting accordingly. We have made less progress in our ability to operate complex systems, which defy conventional modeling and challenge traditional management practices. Leaders need to use better tools for anticipating how these systems will behave—tools that can help us understand the constant interactions of numerous elements and the impact of rare but extreme events. By taking steps to mitigate risks, making measured tradeoffs that keep early failures small, and gathering diverse thinkers who can deal creatively with variation, we can approach decision making in our complex organizations with more confidence and increase our chances of success.

How Complexity Disrupts Business Ecosystems

Many companies that once functioned within simple, self-contained markets now face competition from unexpected players. Consider, for example, the payments business.

Card issuers such as Visa, MasterCard, and American Express make money from two sources: annual cardholder fees and payments from vendors who accept the card. New players, including mobile-telephone operators and technology giants such as Google, are now racing into the payments market.

Because these companies don't need to make money from payments—their business models are supported by advertising—the collateral damage could be considerable. As business ecosystems become more interconnected and thus more complex, this kind of disruption becomes more common and causes more harm.

A Counterintuitive Approach to Hiring

In *The Difference* (Princeton University Press, 2007), Scott E. Page, a social scientist and complex systems expert at the University of Michigan, examines a number of topics relating to diversity. One concerns strategies for hiring people who will maximize the cognitive variety within a company.

Consider the test results below, which represent the responses of three people being considered for two open positions; each X indicates a correct answer. The candidates chosen will join a research team in which diverse thinking is of the utmost importance. Which two would you hire?

Jeff has the highest number of correct answers (7); Rose and Spencer have 6 and 5, respectively. Assuming that everything else is constant, most of us would conclude that Jeff should definitely be hired. You'd probably also hire Rose. Page argues that this might not be the best decision, though. Notice that every question Rose answered correctly was also answered correctly by Jeff; her knowledge is likely to duplicate his. Moreover, although Spencer got the fewest correct answers, he gave the correct answer to every question that Jeff got wrong; he's apt to bring something different to the table. The lesson: If your organization needs people with diverse points of view, your HR strategy should try to complement the Jeffs with the Spencers.

The Idea in Brief

In just a short time, most businesses have gone from complicated to complex: They contain numerous diverse, interdependent parts. This makes managers' jobs much more difficult.

- They can't predict what will happen when various parts of the business interact; the same starting conditions may yield different results.
- Seemingly simple actions produce unintended consequences.
- Human beings' cognitive limits mean that no manager can understand all aspects of the business—but many refuse to acknowledge those limits.
- Rare events can be more significant than average ones—and may occur more often than we think.

Managers can navigate these difficulties by making fundamental changes to how they approach key tasks:

- Forecasting
- Mitigating risks
- Making tradeoffs
- Ensuring diversity of thought

CHAPTER 6

Living in the Futures

How scenario planning changed corporate strategy *by Angela Wilkinson and Roland Kupers*

In 1965 Royal Dutch Shell put into service what it called the Unified Planning Machinery (UPM), a computer-driven system meant to bring more discipline to the company's cash flow planning. This kind of rational, modelbased financial forecasting was very much in vogue in the 1960s. But before long, Shell's top executives realized that many of the commitments they had to make extended well beyond UPM's six-year time horizon—and that even within that horizon, UPM tended to get a lot wrong. In the early 1970s they shut it down.

Things have gone much better for another Shell initiative that was begun in 1965, albeit with far less fanfare. Jimmy Davidson, the head of economics and planning for Shell's exploration and production division, tapped the company veteran Ted Newland to start an activity called Long-Term Studies at the London headquarters. "I was placed in a little cubicle on the 18th floor and told to think about the future, with no real indications of what was required of me," Newland recalls. His appointment marked the start of a remarkable and still ongoing experiment in using scenario planning to engage with an uncertain future.

Under the leadership of Newland and Davidson, who became Shell's first overall head of planning in 1967, the "futures" operation began to take shape. Newland started by delivering a "Year 2000" study report. Then, together with his new colleague Henk Alkema, he began to develop long-term outlooks in the form of alternative futures. The very first oil-price scenarios prepared by this duo were sent to senior executives by mid-1971. Around this time Davidson brought in Pierre Wack, who had been the head of planning for Shell Française, to try to secure the attention and interest of Shell's most senior executives. Wack, a former magazine editor with a bent

for Eastern philosophy and mysticism, focused on telling plausible stories about how the wider business context of Shell might develop. Together with Newland he came to define the practice of scenario planning at Shell; each man headed the team at some point during an eventful decade of oil crises and economic turmoil that they and their colleagues had to some extent envisioned ahead of time. But Shellstyle scenario planning has never really been about predicting the future. Its value lies in how scenarios are embedded in—and provide vital links between organizational processes such as strategy making, innovation, risk management, public affairs, and leadership development. It has helped break the habit, ingrained in most corporate planning, of assuming that the future will look much like the present. As unthreatening stories, scenarios enable Shell executives to open their minds to previously inconceivable or imperceptible developments.

Scenario planning has now been in use at Shell for more than 45 years, spanning times of great triumph and prominence—especially in the 1970s—but also long stretches during which company leaders struggled to see its value. It has come close to being shut down at least three times. But it has continued to evolve and help shape the company's global thinking about energy and other matters—and, at times, its strategy. For an operation that doesn't contribute directly to the bottom line, and that emphasizes the uncertainty of the future rather than making bold predictions, this is remarkable.

The practice is also enjoying a renaissance outside Shell, with growing evidence of its effectiveness. A recent survey of 77 large companies by René Rohrbeck, of Aarhus University, and Jan Oliver Schwarz, of Germany's EBS Business School, found that formal "strategic foresight" efforts add value through (1) an enhanced capacity to perceive change, (2) an enhanced capacity to interpret and respond to change, (3) influence on other actors, and (4) an enhanced capacity for organizational learning. Two Bain researchers reported in 2007 that the firm's regular survey of management tools showed "an abrupt and sustained surge" in the use of scenario planning after 9/11, and although there have been ups and downs since, Bain's most recent survey showed that 65% of companies expected to use scenario planning in 2011.

Credit for originating scenario planning often goes to the American game theorist and futurist Herman Kahn. However, a form of the practice emerged simultaneously in France in the work of Gaston Berger, Bertrand de Jouvenel, and others. The American approach came to emphasize probability, with degrees of likelihood assigned to various outcomes, while the French approach focused more on what *should* happen. Newland and Wack, aware of both, steered clear of probabilistic forecasts and normative statements and instead insisted that scenarios should first and foremost be *plausible*. One U.S. government report from a decade ago estimated that 85% of the scenario studies surveyed by the report's authors were based on or derived from the Royal Dutch Shell process, suggesting that Shell's experience contains lessons relevant for anyone—investors, corporations, governments, nongovernmental organizations, and others—trying to engage with the future.

We are a former Shell scenario planner and a former Shell executive who recently completed a history of scenario planning at the company after interviewing almost every surviving veteran of the operation, along with current and former top company executives. With help from Betty Sue Flowers, who edited several Shell scenarios in the 1990s, we discovered that although the practice has evolved over the decades, we can identify the principles that both define the process at Shell and help explain how it has survived and thrived for so long.

Make It Plausible, Not Probable

But, of course, you can never identify all the forces at play. If you could, and see their interactions, then real prediction of the future would be simple. This is never likely to be possible, and furthermore, there are some situations that balance on a hair's breadth.—Jimmy Davidson, head of group planning 1967–1976

From the beginning, those engaged with Shell's scenario practice maintained that scenarios are not predictions but can provide a deeper foundation of knowledge and self-awareness in approaching the future. They also felt that the "official" view of the future—the business-as-usual outlook—both reflects an optimism bias and is based on the human tendency to see familiar patterns and be blind to the unexpected.

In the late 1960s Shell's business-as-usual approach was embodied by UPM and its quantitative, model-based methodology, which some worried was likely to suppress discussion rather than to encourage a healthy exchange of differing perspectives. Deductive methods for generating scenarios—for example, a 2x2 matrix with axes for public/private and more-expensive/less-expensive—were never core to the Shell practice, although they are often identified with it because Peter Schwartz, who ran the scenario team in the early 1980s, subsequently promoted their use at the strategy consulting group Global Business Network. In general, the company has also avoided expressing a preference for one scenario over another. The trap of having a "good" versus a "bad" future is that there is nothing to learn in heaven, and no one wants to visit hell.

The Shell method instead emphasized plausibility. During the early years of experimentation, Wack encouraged his team to consider any scenario as long as it could not be rendered implausible through logical reasoning. Later he decided that approach generated too many scenarios to be effective. But the focus on plausibility remained. Shell scenarios are intended to set the stage for a future world in which readers imagine themselves as actors and are invited to pay attention to deeply held assumptions about how that world works. What happens at a scenario's horizon date is not as important as the storyline's clarity of logic and how it helps open the mind to new dynamics.

Plausible stories encourage judgment, not just attention to data and other information. By acknowledging that subjective judgment and intuition are an integral part of the leadership process, scenarios create a safe space in which to acknowledge uncertainty. An intuitive understanding of the world precedes and frames the analytical understanding that follows. Intuition is the essence of entrepreneurial value creation, and it can be stifled by a paralysis of analysis.

Plausibility can be strengthened by how relevant and memorable the scenario is, as well as by a logical story line. In the mid-1980s Lo van Wachem, the chairman of Shell's committee of managing directors, instructed the scenario team to begin considering the impact of sustainability concerns on the energy business. The process took years, but it ended up shaping opinion throughout the group as the threat of global warming became more real. Shell's 1998 sustainability report was one of the first acknowledgments by a major energy corporation of the challenge of climate change.

Strike a Balance Between Relevant and Challenging

All successful scenarios are focused in the sense that they are derived from a fundamental consideration of their client's dilemmas and needs. —Ged Davis, head of the scenario team 1999–2003

Shell's scenario practice started out by exposing and questioning the official version of the future. This was especially important because of the company's decentralized nature: Until 2005 Shell had two parent companies (one British, one Dutch) and two headquarters (one in London, one in the Hague). Its country operations around the world enjoyed striking autonomy. It was led not by a CEO but by a committee of managing directors (CMD). As a result, consensus was crucial, and to a large extent the corporate view of the future was implicit and unarticulated—and thus particularly hard to change.

Scenarios facilitated dialogue in which managers' assumptions could safely be revealed and challenged. They enabled consideration of unexpected developments—such as the chairman's sustainability agenda in the 1980s—and inconvenient truths, such as OPEC's power over oil prices in the 1970s. They encouraged strategic conversations that went beyond the incremental, comfortable, and familiar progression customary in a consensus culture. Many business units, and corporate functions beyond strategy and finance, went on to develop scenarios.

To seize and retain the attention of all these constituencies, though, Shell's scenarios had to be more than disruptive and challenging; they had to be *relevant* to executives, from the CMD on down. In the early days, global events conspired to make them so. Scenarios prepared in 1971 and 1972 sketched the possibility that the power in oil markets would shift from consumers to oil-producing nations—and that the interests of those producers would dictate cuts in production, not the eternal increases foreseen in the business-as-usual version of the future. After subsequent scenarios in 1973 deemed business-as-usual implausible, and a Mideast oil embargo and global energy crisis followed mere months later, there was no questioning the relevance of this work.

In the 1980s, though, Shell's top management largely ignored the plausible and challenging scenarios of global economic growth and power shifts. The reasons that have been offered for this range from a failure of the scenario team to listen to the concerns of executives to an overemphasis on bigpicture developments as opposed to the energy industry and Shell in particular. Kees van der Heijden, who took over as scenario chief in 1988, decided that extensive interviews with Shell leaders were needed to ensure that the scenarios addressed relevant issues. "Deep listening" through structured interviews soon became standard practice; interview questions probed the core concerns of decision makers and their hopes for the future and uncovered uncertainties about the company, its business, and its environment. Van der Heijden's successor, Joseph Jaworski, spent his first six months on the job conducting more than 100 one-on-one interviews with Shell executives that lasted three or four hours each. This approach continued and has been effective: Despite the challenging and uncomfortable nature of many scenarios, only rarely have Shell leaders dismissed them as irrelevant or too dangerous to share (although rewrites have sometimes been requested).

To stay relevant, the scenarios have had to change. The early ones were designed to open up executive thinking in an environment in which oil companies had long been logistical machines that saw no need to communicate with one another or to focus on external events. Demand was assumed to be predictable, and the main job was to get oil to the customer as efficiently as possible. This was the context in which Wack "opened the company to the outside world," as Van der Heijden puts it.

Since then the global energy business has transformed Shell from a strategic player that produced 10% of the world's oil and gas before the 1970s crises to just one of many large energy companies (it produces less than 2% today). The organization's structure has also changed: Formerly a one-of-a-kind dual-nationality company with roots in the colonial past, it is now a more conventional multinational with a CEO at the top and a focus on shareholder returns. As a result, recent Shell scenarios have been more concerned with energy than with social and economic issues and have been more broadly institutionalized so as to have an impact on corporate decision making. As the current CEO, Peter Voser, says, "We have maintained intellectual agility and operational flexibility by shifting beyond global to more 'sliced and diced' scenarios."

It remains difficult to strike an appropriate balance between relevant and challenging. Relevant can be too familiar, but challenging can go unheard. As Wack once said, "You take the piece of bread and you put it in front of the goldfish, but not so far that the goldfish can't get it."

Tell Stories That Are Memorable Yet Disposable

You are trying to manipulate people into being open-minded. —Ted Newland, manager of Long-Term Studies 1965–1971; scenario team leader 1980–1981

Corporations, like human beings, act on the basis of an agreed-upon reality—which is, in essence, a story. Stories of the past and the present can be based on facts, but a story of the future is *just* a story. The problem is that the stories we most commonly tell about the future simply extrapolate from the present.

Perhaps the greatest power of scenarios, as distinct from forecasts, is that they consciously break this habit. They introduce discontinuities so that conversations about strategy—which lie at the heart of any organization's capacity to adapt—can encompass something different from the present.

Storytelling is key to making this process work. A story is not a position, so no one has to be for or against it or line up behind the CEO's opinion. If it's sufficiently vivid and memorable, it allows executives to discuss difficult issues without having to revisit arguments connected with them: A few words can evoke a world. Charismatic presenters; evocative graphics; memorable phrases, images, and archetypes; illustrative graphs of future outlooks; and the preparation of the audience through interviews, workshops, and other forms of participation all contribute to the storytelling power of Shell's scenarios.

In the early years, the Shell team developed sets of six or seven scenarios. By the mid-1970s three scenarios were common, but that tempted managers to choose a "middle way" as a best guess. Starting in 1989, two scenarios became the norm, enhancing usability and recall. Two stories open the mind but don't numb it with too many variables. In addition to these, some more-focused scenarios—on a project, a country, a crisis, a market entry, or an investment decision, for example—were often developed throughout the organization.

Scenarios have a limited shelf life. As they become familiar, the temptation arises to cling to them—which risks thinking within, rather than looking beyond, the box. Generating new scenarios on an ongoing basis counters the tendency to hold on to familiar ones. Over the past decade, Shell has abandoned its former practice of creating them according to a regular rhythm and shifted toward updating, discarding, or building new ones on an as-needed basis. Thus the scenarios act as temporary scaffolding—rather than a fixed structure—to support the strategic conversation.

Add Numbers to Narrative

Engineers are numbers people, and if you can't quantify what you are talking about, they tend to dismiss you as interesting (at best) mystics. —DeAnne Julius, Shell's chief economist 1993–1997

As noted, Shell's scenario practice developed partly out of dissatisfaction with mechanistic, modelbased projections. Scenarios were meant to harness intuition, not fall back on numbers. Wack, says his longtime colleague Napier Collyns, "regarded computer modeling as the enemy of thought."

Yet Collyns, who served on the scenario team from 1972 to 1986, frequently used numbers and computer models. Shell's scenarios have never been developed from mechanistic modeling, but they have always been associated with quantification to enhance internal consistency, reveal deep story logic and systemic insight, and illustrate outcomes using the language of numbers that characterizes most corporate cultures.

In the early years of the scenario practice, Collyns and Harry Beckers—who later became Shell's head of research—supported quantification despite Wack's limited appetite for it. Peter Schwartz later experimented with computer models linked to scenarios as a means of encouraging serious learning through "play." In the 2001 scenario round, two econometric models were used after the global scenarios had been developed to quantify the implications for GDP growth of various patterns of oil and gas price coupling, decoupling, and volatility.

During preparation of the 2007 long-term energy scenarios, the team built a comprehensive world energy model that simulated the development of the energy market over decades. It allowed the team to explore a much wider range of what-ifs by tweaking a large number of inputs, including the energy efficiency of electrical appliances, the depreciation time of coal-fired power plants, and shifts in consumer behavior.

Of course, large-scale quantitative models require considerable investment, which can lead to a kind of "model lock-in": Difficulty in changing basic assumptions, along with the natural authority of algorithmic calculations, can result in users' being blindsided by changes in the world that don't fit a model's parameters. In the few years following publication of the 2007 scenarios, at least three major energy-market events failed to fit the world energy model: the 2008 financial crisis; the U.S. shale-gas boom; and Germany's decision, after the Fukushima nuclear disaster, to speed up its transition to renewables. However, the model *had* been used to trace the energy impact of a deep recession—giving credibility to the recession-and-recovery scenarios that were created and presented to Shell's executive committee within days of the Lehman Brothers collapse in 2008.

Quantification is essential to scenarios. The challenge lies in realizing how, when, and why models linked with them can hide assumptions and constrain thinking rather than refine it. If, for example, Shell begins to rely on its state-of-the-art global energy model to provide what-if analysis, the signature advantage of scenarios in reframing thinking will be weakened. But used as a secondary tool, a quantitative model can fortify a rapid-response scenario. The persuasive power of scenarios in the world of business rests on an effective combination of narrative and numbers.

Scenarios Open Doors

We facilitated a set of scenarios for the Chinese government. The notion that you would actually think outside the official plan was like pulling teeth. Over a one-year period we developed the scenarios with them, and it gives you insights into the way they are thinking that you just can't get otherwise and, of course, you wouldn't get as a businessperson across the table discussing things with them. —Doug McKay, scenario team member 1996–2002

Over time, agreement appears to have been unanimous that scenarios are valuable in external engagement. Shell has used global scenarios to add color to corporate speeches, to open doors to privileged conversations with resource holders and governments, and to build a network of NGO contacts. Since 1992 it has released smaller, public versions of its global scenarios—after enough time has passed for the company to gain competitive advantage from internal digestion and use. But more important has been the way scenarios have created value through new business development, joint venturing, and new market entry. Building scenarios with key stakeholders in prospective joint projects has enabled an invaluable exchange of perspectives and insights. Shell has developed focused scenarios for state oil companies in, for example, Brunei, Kuwait, Nigeria, and Oman.

Members of the scenario team have also occasionally shared their expertise. For example, since the 1980s, when a remarkable body of unpublished scenario work on greater China was started by one of their number, team members have been involved in a variety of scenario initiatives focused on energy, sustainable development, and other concerns relevant to the Chinese government. In 1991 one team member assisted in creating scenarios that helped focus the attention of both the African National Congress and the De Klerk government on the importance of economic development during South Africa's messy political transition. Another led a 1998 effort to develop global scenarios covering 2000–2050 for the World Business Council for Sustainable Development, which highlighted alternative models for thinking about progress. In 2005 yet another helped build scenarios for UNAIDS that exposed difficult choices between prevention and treatment and care. Shell's scenario experts often contributed to other efforts after leaving the company—starting with Wack, who participated in scenario rounds in South Africa in the 1980s.

Manage Disagreement as an Asset

In hindsight, the greatest value of scenarios is that they created a culture where you could ask anyone a question, and the answer would need to be contextual. Answering "Because I'm the boss" or "Because the business case is positive" was out-of-bounds. —Ted Newland

Scenarios have the power to engage and open the minds of decision makers so that they pay attention to novel, less comfortable, and weaker signals of change and prepare for discontinuity and surprise. When the oil crisis of October 1973 hit, Shell's committee of managing directors had already considered a comparable scenario. As one scenario team member put it, "And then, of course, high oil prices came, and everybody said, 'You're very clever, you've got that right.' And we all said, 'No, wrong. We're not forecasters. We're your 'personal trainers.'"

Under Shell's earlier, decentralized structure, scenarios provided a common learning culture, helped create a shared view of the world, and refreshed the strategic agenda, enabling new concepts, such as resilience (1970s), sustainable development (1989), and systemic risk (2002), to penetrate the organization. They were a steering tool for the CMD and served as corporate glue to hold the organization together. As Shell became more centralized, scenarios provided a way to manage disagreement about group strategy or priorities and helped disturb the business-as-usual view that tends to result from wishful thinking or the linear extrapolation of current trends.

Within the CMD, scenarios also became a mediation tool. Given that the committee did not vote things into effect but recommended them for formal approval by the boards of the parent companies, scenarios were a unifying force. They redirected attention and encouraged dialogue rather than prescribing action, which made them nonthreatening.

Fit into a Broader Strategic Management System

Scenarios provide the right framework for appreciating fundamental long-term choice, which is not the same as next year's annual plan. —Peter Voser, Shell's CEO 2009–

Living in the Futures

In one of a series of retirement presentations to Shell's CMD in 1981 and 1982, Pierre Wack borrowed a phrase from the organizational theorist Russell Ackoff: "corporate rain dance." This is a ritual that happens at a given time of the year, when the strategic planning process is rolled out. "It has no impact whatsoever on the weather, but everything that comes afterwards is nicely linked to and explained by this rain dance," Wack said. "And some people enjoy it very much." Wack was convinced that creativity could be institutionalized in corporate strategic planning, avoiding the rain dance. And he believed that scenarios, because they follow a rhythm distinct from the annual strategy cycle, allow an organization to see realities that might otherwise be overlooked.

Wack identified three essential starting points for corporate strategy: global scenarios, competitive positioning, and strategic vision. The first represents the world of possibility, the second the world of relativity, and the third the world of creativity. The challenge in effective scenario work is to go beyond the usual strategic focus on current trends and competitive positioning (profitability, for example) to find the right scale of observation. The next challenge is to look for some degree of fit between the company's core capabilities and the variety of plausible future conditions.

Wack argued that strategic vision is not driven top-down by a corporate leader but involves a capacity to ask the right questions and to be amazed. He saw the organization as an animal that can prosper within a particular habitat. The success of the strategic vision thus depends on matching capabilities and context. Scenarios can help that vision evolve and become a source of dynamism.

THE MOST common question about Shell's scenario practice is "Did it work?" That is, did it create direct business value by enabling better decisions? The answer is "yes" in the case of more-focused scenarios and "only indirectly" in the case of global scenarios. We have no solid examples of Shell's having anticipated future developments better than other companies—the mythology around anticipation of the 1970s oil crises notwithstanding. The historian Keetie Sluyterman characterizes Shell as being perhaps faster than other companies in catching on to changes in market or culture, by virtue of its sensitivity to emerging topics such as climate change, the rise of China, and the controversial boom in the development of extensive unconventional gas resources in the United States.

How can anyone determine in advance if one decision is better than another? In contrast to decision theory, which assumes that all outcomes can be known, scenarios encourage attention to the future's openness and irreducible uncertainty. Success in the future depends on the future success of decisions, which can't be known in advance. The outcome is at best a hypothesis rather than a range or a precise data point.

What does seem clear is that a sustained scenario practice can make leaders comfortable with the ambiguity of an open future. It can counter hubris, expose assumptions that would otherwise remain implicit, contribute to shared and systemic sensemaking, and foster quick adaptation in times of crisis. Scenarios can build social capital within and beyond the organization. They can aid in navigating complexity and conflict—managing disagreement while avoiding the extremes of groupthink and fragmentation. At Shell and elsewhere, scenarios have helped leaders prepare for futures that *might* happen, rather than the future they would like to create.

Stories of the Future

The first formal round of Shell scenarios was completed in November 1971. Since then Shell's scenario planners have produced 34 rounds of global and long-term energy scenarios and updates and many more-focused ones. Some synopsized examples are included here and on the following pages, under the actual Shell titles.

Shell scenarios 1973

- **"Crisis Scenario"** A late response to an impending energy gap causes oil prices to spiral upward. Producer governments exert tight control on the industry through nationalization.
- **"Dirigiste Solution"** The governments of consumer nations intervene in energy markets, supported by public opinion. The energy industry gets subsidies, constraints are imposed on consumption, and conservation is encouraged.

Shell scenarios 1977

- **"Carter Miracle"** The moral leadership exuded by U.S. President Jimmy Carter restores confidence. Governments take measures to strengthen international trade and investment.
- **"Convalescence"** Recovery is slower than normal. Unemployment combines with a dim view of government in general to make the system fragile.
- **"Relapse"** Inflation rises sharply, as do wages. The global economy is buffeted by conflict in the Middle East and other external shocks.

Shell scenarios 1989

- **"Global Merc antilism"** Economic power is the driving force. Conflicting regional interests affect economic security and the environment. Protectionism grows, and trade is managed through bilateral agreements. Many developing countries are left behind.
- **"Sustainable World"** The environment dominates the agenda. The global economic system is resilient, and developing countries are brought on board. Growth in the energy business is limited. An emphasis on clean fuels leads to a reconstruction of the industry.

Shell scenarios 1995

- **"Just Do It!"** Success comes to those who harness the latest innovations in technology to take advantage of quick-moving opportunities in a world of hypercompetition, customization, self-reliance, and informal networking.
- **"Da Wo"** (Chinese for "Big Me") Countries and companies discover that relationships of trust and the enabling role of government provide long-term strategic advantage. This favors Asia, because its people and businesses view individual and societal welfare as inextricably linked.

Shell scenarios 2001

- **"Business Class"** A globally interconnected elite and the only remaining superpower lead the world toward greater economic integration and prosperity. Cities and other power centers diminish the influence of national governments and unleash a "new medievalism."
- **"Prism"** The persistent power of culture and history shape a "new regionalism," putting the monochromatic world of global integration in question.

CHAPTER 7

Adaptability: The New Competitive Advantage

In a world of constant change, the spoils go to the nimble. by Martin Reeves and Mike Deimler

We live in an era of risk and instability. Globalization, new technologies, and greater transparency have combined to upend the business environment and give many CEOs a deep sense of unease. Just look at the numbers. Since 1980 the volatility of business operating margins, largely static since the 1950s, has more than doubled, as has the size of the gap between winners (companies with high operating margins) and losers (those with low ones).

Market leadership is even more precarious. The percentage of companies falling out of the top three rankings in their industry increased from 2% in 1960 to 14% in 2008. What's more, market leadership is proving to be an increasingly dubious prize: The once strong correlation between profitability and industry share is now almost nonexistent in some sectors. According to our calculation, the probability that the market share leader is also the profitability leader declined from 34% in 1950 to just 7% in 2007. And it has become virtually impossible for some executives even to clearly identify in what industry and with which companies they're competing.

All this uncertainty poses a tremendous challenge for strategy making. That's because traditional approaches to strategy—though often seen as theanswer to change and uncertainty—actually assume a relatively stable and predictable world.

Think about it. The goal of most strategies is to build an enduring (and implicitly static) competitive advantage by establishing clever market positioning (dominant scale or an attractive niche) or assembling the right capabilities and competencies for making or delivering an offering (doing what the company does well). Companies undertake periodic strategy reviews and set direction and organizational structure on the basis of an analysis of their industry and some forecast of how it will evolve.

But given the new level of uncertainty, many companies are starting to ask:

- How can we apply frameworks that are based on scale or position when we can go from market leader one year to follower the next?

- When it's unclear where one industry ends and another begins, how do we even measure position?

- When the environment is so unpredictable, how can we apply the traditional forecasting and analysis that are at the heart of strategic planning?

- When we're overwhelmed with changing information, how can our managers pick up the right signals to understand and harness change?

- When change is so rapid, how can a one-year—or, worse, five-year—planning cycle stay relevant?

The answers these companies are coming up with point in a consistent direction. Sustainable competitive advantage no longer arises exclusively from position, scale, and first-order capabilities in producing or delivering an offering. All those are essentially static. So where does it come from? Increasingly, managers are finding that it stems from the "second-order"

49

organizational capabilities that foster rapid adaptation. Instead of being really good at doing some particular thing, companies must be really good at learning how to do new things.

Those that thrive are quick to read and act on signals of change. They have worked out how to experiment rapidly, frequently, and economically—not only with products and services but also with business models, processes, and strategies. They have built up skills in managing complex multistakeholder systems in an increasingly interconnected world. Perhaps most important, they have learned to unlock their greatest resources—the people who work for them. In the following pages we'll look at how companies at the leading edge are using these four organizational capabilities to attain adaptive advantage. We'll also discuss the implications of this fundamental strategic shift for large, established corporations, many of which have built their operations around scale and efficiency—sources of advantage that rely on an essentially stable environment.

The Ability to Read and Act on Signals

In order to adapt, a company must have its antennae tuned to signals of change from the external environment, decode them, and quickly act to refine or reinvent its business model and even reshape the information landscape of its industry.

Think back to when Stirling Moss was winning Formula One car races: The car and the driver determined who won. But today the sport is as much about processing complex signals and making adaptive decisions as about mechanics and driving prowess. Hundreds of sensors are built into the cars; race teams continuously collect and process data on several thousand variables—ranging from weather and road conditions to engine rpm and the angles of curves—and feed them into dynamic simulation models that guide the drivers' split-second decisions. A telemetric innovation by one team can instantly raise the bar for all.

In this information-saturated age, when complex, varying signals may be available simultaneously to all players, adaptive companies must similarly rely on sophisticated point-of-sale systems to ensure that they acquire the right information. And they must apply advanced data-mining technologies to recognize relevant patterns in it.

For example, a leading media company that was suffering from a high rate of customer churn revamped its analytic approach to customer data, applying "neural network" technologies in order to understand patterns of customer loss. The company found hidden relationships among the variables that were driving churn and launched retention campaigns targeting at-risk customers. The accuracy rate in predicting churn was an impressive 75% to 90%—a huge benefit, given that every percentage point in churn reduction added millions of dollars to the bottom line.

Companies are also leveraging their signal-reading capabilities to make operational interventions in real time, bypassing slow-moving decision hierarchies. The UK-based grocery retailer Tesco continually performs detailed analyses of the purchase patterns of the more than 13 million members of its loyalty-card program. Its findings enable Tesco to customize offerings for each store and each customer segment and provide early warning of shifts in customer behavior. They also supported the development of Tesco's hugely successful online platform, which has extended the company's business model, enabling Tesco to become a store without walls and to offer a broader range of products and services, including media and financial services. To put the icing on the cake, instead of being purely a cost center, the rich databases and analytical capabilities produce a stream of direct revenue: For a fee, Tesco allows other enterprises to access its technologies and insights.

Google is another example. It uses algorithms to update the position of an ad on the basis of the ad's relevance to an individual search or website as well as the advertiser's bids on key words. The more relevant an ad, the higher the click-through rate—and because advertisers pay per click, this means more revenue for Google. By linking its advertising data directly to its operations, Google can respond to changing ad conditions on a split-second basis, without the intervention of human decision makers.

The Ability to Experiment

That which cannot be deduced or forecast can often be discovered through experimentation. Of course, all companies use some form of experimentation to develop and test new products and services. Yet the traditional approaches can be costly and time-consuming, and may saddle the organization with an unreasonable burden of complexity. Furthermore, research based on consumers' perceptions is often a remarkably poor predictor of success. The real world is an expensive medium for experimentation, and failed market-facing tests and pilots may jeopardize a company's brand and reputation.

To overcome these barriers, a growing number of adaptive competitors are using an array of new approaches and technologies, especially in virtual environments, to generate, test, and replicate a larger number of innovative ideas faster, at lower cost, and with less risk than their rivals can. Procter & Gamble is a case in point. Through its Connect +Develop model, it leverages InnoCentive and other open-innovation networks to solve technical design problems. It uses a walk-in, 3-D virtual store to run experiments that are quicker and cheaper than traditional market tests. And by employing Vocalpoint and other online user communities, it can introduce and test products with friendly audiences before a full launch. In 2008 alone, 10 highly skilled employees were able to generate some 10,000 design simulations, enabling the completion in hours of mock-ups that might once have taken weeks. More than 80% of P&G's new-business initiatives now make use of its growing virtual toolbox.

In addition to changing the way in which they conduct experiments, companies need to broaden the scope of their experimentation. Traditionally, the focus has been on a company's offerings essentially new products and services. But in an increasingly turbulent environment, business models, strategies, and routines can also become obsolete quickly and unpredictably. Adaptive companies therefore use experimentation far more broadly than their rivals do. We've seen that Tesco illustrates the power of experimenting with business models as well as with product range.

Ikea, like Tesco, leverages existing assets and capabilities to experiment with business models. After the company entered Russia, managers noticed that whenever it opened a store, the value of nearby real estate increased dramatically. So Ikea decided to explore two business models simultaneously: retailing through its stores and capturing the appreciation in real estate values through mall development. It now makes more profit in Russia from developing and operating malls than from its traditional retail business.

Finally, experimentation necessarily produces failure. Adaptive companies are very tolerant of failure, even to the point of celebrating it. For example, the software company Intuit, which has been extremely successful at using adaptive approaches to grow new businesses, launched a marketing campaign in 2005 to reach young tax filers through a website called rockyourrefund.com. The site offered discounts at Expedia and Best Buy and the opportunity to get tax refunds in the form of prepaid gift cards. The campaign was a flop, and practically no one used the site. The amount of money involved was negligible—"almost a rounding error," says Rick Jensen, the vice president of product management for Intuit's consumer tax division. But the marketing team documented what it had learned from the failure and won an award from company chairman Scott Cook, who said, "It is only a failure if we fail to get the learning."

The Ability to Manage Complex Multicompany Systems

Signal detection and experimentation require a company to think beyond its own boundaries and perhaps to work more closely and smartly with customers and suppliers. This flies somewhat in the face of the unspoken assumption that the unit of analysis for strategy is a single company or business unit.

With an increasing amount of economic activity occurring beyond corporate boundaries—through outsourcing, offshoring, value nets, value ecosystems, peer production, and the like—we need to think about strategies not only for individual companies but also for dynamic business systems. Increasingly, industry structure is better characterized as competing webs or ecosystems of codependent companies than as a handful of competitors producing similar goods and services and working on a stable, distant, and transactional basis with their suppliers and customers.

In such an environment advantage will flow to those companies that can create effective strategies at the network or system level. Adaptive companies are therefore learning how to push activities outside the company without benefiting competitors and how to design and evolve strategies for networks without necessarily being able to rely on strong control mechanisms.

Typically, adaptive companies manage their ecosystems by using common standards to foster interaction with minimal barriers. They generate trust among participants—for example, by enabling people to interact frequently and by providing transparency and rating systems that serve as "reputational currency." Toyota's automotive supply pyramids, with their *kanban* and *kaizen* feedback mechanisms, are early examples of adaptive systems. EBay's complex network of sellers and buyers is another; the company relies on seller ratings and online payment systems to support the online marketplace.

If the experience curve and the scale curve were the key indicators of success, Nokia would still be leading the smartphone market; it had the advantage of being an early mover and the market share leader with a strong cost position. But Nokia was attacked by an entirely different kind of competitor: Apple's adaptive system of suppliers, telecom partnerships, and numerous independent application developers, created to support the iPhone. Google's Android operating system, too, capitalized on a broad array of hardware partners and application developers. The ability to bring together the assets and capabilities of so many entities allowed these smartphone entrants to leapfrog the experience curve and become new market leaders in record time. As Stephen Elop, Nokia's CEO, wrote in a memo to his staff, "Our competitors aren't taking our market share with devices; they are taking our market share with an entire ecosystem." Through broader signal detection, parallel innovation, superior flexibility, and rapid mobilization, multicompany systems can enhance the adaptiveness of individual companies.

The Ability to Mobilize

Adaptation is necessarily local in nature—somebody experiments first at a particular place and time. It is also necessarily global in nature, because if the experiment succeeds, it will be communicated, selected, amplified, and refined. Organizations therefore need to create environments that encourage the knowledge flow, diversity, autonomy, risk taking, sharing, and flexibility on which adaptation thrives. Contrary to classical strategic thinking, strategy follows organization in adaptive companies.

A flexible structure and the dispersal of decision rights are powerful levers for increasing adaptability. Typically, adaptive companies have replaced permanent silos and functions with modular units that freely communicate and recombine according to the situation at hand. To reinforce this framework, it is helpful to have weak or competing power structures and a culture of constructive conflict and dissent. Cisco is one company that has made this transformation. Early on, it relied on a hierarchical, customercentric organization to become a leader in the market for network switches and routers. More recently the CEO, John Chambers, has created a novel management structure of cross-functional councils and boards to facilitate moves into developing countries and 30 adjacent and diverse markets (ranging from health care to sports) with greater agility than would previously have been possible.

As they create more-fluid structures, adaptive companies drive decision making down to the front lines, allowing the people most likely to detect changes in the environment to respond quickly and proactively. For example, at Whole Foods the basic organizational unit is the team, and each store has about eight teams. Team leaders—not national buyers—decide what to stock. Teams have veto power over new hires. They are encouraged to buy from local growers that meet the company's quality and sustainability standards. And they are rewarded for their performance with bonuses based on store profitability over the previous four weeks.

Creating decentralized, fluid, and even competing organizational structures destroys the big advantage of a rigid hierarchy, which is that everyone knows precisely what he or she should be doing. An adaptive organization can't expect to succeed unless it provides people with some substitute for that certainty. What's needed is some simple, generative rules to facilitate interaction, help people make trade-offs, and set the boundaries within which they can make decisions.

For example, Netflix values nine core behaviors and skills in its employees: judgment, communication, impact, curiosity, innovation, courage, passion, honesty, and selflessness. The company's executives believe that a great workplace is full of "stunning colleagues" who embody these qualities; thus the Netflix model is to "increase employee freedom aswe grow, rather than limit it, to continue to attract and nourish innovative people, so we have a better chance of long-term continued success." Consistent with this philosophy, Netflix has only two types of rules: those designed to prevent irrevocable disaster and those designed to prevent moral, ethical, and legal issues. It has no vacation policy and does no tracking of time—the company's focus is on what needs to get done, not how many hours or days are worked. As the Netflix "Reference Guide on Our Freedom & Responsibility Culture" puts it, "Avoid Chaos as you grow with Ever More High Performance People—not with Rules."

The Challenge for Big Business

Becoming an adaptive competitor can be difficult, especially for large, established organizations. Typically, these companies are oriented toward managing scale and efficiency, and their hierarchical structures and fixed routines lack the diversity and flexibility needed for rapid learning and change. Such management paradigms die hard, especially when they have historically been the basis for success.

However, several tactics have proved effective at fostering adaptive advantage even in established companies. To the managers involved, they may look like nothing more than an extension of business as usual, but in fact they create a context in which adaptive capabilities can thrive. If you are the CEO of a large company that wants to be more adaptive, challenge your managers to:

Look at the mavericks. Fast-changing industries are characterized by the presence of disruptive mavericks often entirely new players, sometimes from other sectors. Ask your managers to shift their focus from traditional competitors' moves to what the new players are doing and to think of ways to insure your company against this new competition or neutralize its effect. They should also look at what's happening in adjacent or analogous industries and markets and ask, "What if this happened in mine?" Although pattern recognition is harder in an uncertain environment and can easily be obstructed by entrenched beliefs and narrow industry definitions, it has tremendous competitive value.

Identify and address the uncertainties. Get your managers to put aside the traditional singlebusiness forecast and instead examine the risks and uncertainties that could significantly affect the company. This simple extension of the familiar longrange strategy exercise can force people to realize what they don't yet know and to address it. Your organization needs to distinguish "false knowns" (questionable but firmly held assumptions) from "underexploited knowns" (megatrends you may recognize and perhaps have even acted on, but without sufficient speed or emphasis) and "unknown unknowns" (intrinsic uncertainties that you can prepare for only by hedging your bets).

Put an initiative on every risk. Most companies have a portfolio of strategic initiatives. It should become the engine that drives your organization into adaptability and it can, with a couple of simple enhancements. First, every significant source of uncertainty should be addressed with an initiative. Depending on the nature of the uncertainty, the goal of the initiative may be responding to a neglected business trend, creating options for responding to it down the line, or simply learning more about it. In managing these initiatives, your company should be as disciplined with metrics, time frames, and responsibilities as it would be for the product portfolio or the operating plan.

Examine multiple alternatives. In a stable environment it is sufficient to improve what already exists or to examine single change proposals. The simple step of requiring that every change proposal be accompanied by several alternatives not only surfaces a more varied and powerful set of moves, but also legitimizes and fosters cognitive diversity and organizational flexibility.

Increase the clock speed. The speed of adaptation is a function of the cycle time of decision making. In a fast-moving environment, companies need to accelerate change by making annual planning processes lighter and more frequent and sometimes by making episodic processes continual.

The adaptive approach is no universal panacea. If your industry is stable and relatively predictable, you may be better off sticking to the traditional sources of advantage. But if your competitive reality is uncertain and rapidly changing, as is true in an increasing number of industries, you need a dynamic and sustainable way to stay ahead. Your survival may depend on building an organization that can exploit the four capabilities behind what we think of as adaptive advantage.

The Idea in Brief

Traditional approaches to strategy assume a relatively stable world. They aim to build an enduring competitive advantage by achieving dominant scale, occupying an attractive niche, or exploiting certain capabilities and resources. But globalization, new technologies, and greater transparency have combined to upend the business environment. Sustainable competitive advantage no longer arises from positioning or resources. Instead, it stems from the four organizational capabilities that foster rapid adaptation:

- The ability to read and act on signals of change
- The ability to experiment rapidly and frequently—not only with products and services but also with business models, processes, and strategies
- The ability to manage complex and interconnected systems of multiple stakeholders
- The ability to motivate employees and partners

CHAPTER 8
Creating Shared Value

How to reinvent capitalism and unleash a wave of innovation and growth by Michael E. Porter and Mark R. Kramer

The capitalist system is under siege. In recent years business increasingly has been viewed as a major cause of social, environmental, and economic problems. Companies are widely perceived to be prospering at the expense of the broader community.

Even worse, the more business has begun to embrace corporate responsibility, the more it has been blamed for society's failures. The legitimacy of business has fallen to levels not seen in recent history. This diminished trust in business leads political leaders to set policies that undermine competitiveness and sap economic growth. Business is caught in a vivious circle.

A big part oft he problem lies with companies themselves, which remain trapped in an outdated approach to value creation that has emerged over the past few decades. They continue to view value creation narrowly, optimizing short-term financial performance in a bubble while missing the most important customer needs and ignoring the broader influences that determine their longer-term success.

How else could companies overlook the wellbeing of their customers, the depletion of natural resources vital to their businesses, the viability of key suppliers, or the economic distress of the communities in which they produce and sell? How else could companies think that simply shifting activities to locations with ever lower wages was a sustainable "solution" to competitive challenges? Government and civil society have often exacerbated the problem by attempting to address social weaknesses at the expense of business. The presumed trade-offs between economic efficiency and social progress have been institutionalized in decades of policy choices.

Companies must take the lead in bringing business and society back together. The recognition is there among sophisticated business and thought leaders, and promising elements of a new model are emerging. Yet we still lack an overall framework for guiding these efforts, and most companies remain stuck in a "social responsibility" mind-set in which societal issues are at the periphery, not the core.

The solution lies in the principle of shared value, which involves creating economic value in a way that *also* creates value for society by addressing its needs and challenges. Businesses must reconnect company success with social progress. Shared value is not social responsibility, philanthropy, or even sustainability, but a new way to achieve economic success. It is not on the margin of what companies do but at the center. We believe that it can give rise to the next major transformation of business thinking.

A growing number of companies known for their hard-nosed approach to business—such as GE, Google, IBM, Intel, Johnson & Johnson, Nestlé, Unilever, and Wal-Mart—have already embarked on important efforts to create shared value by reconceiving the intersection between society and corporate performance. Yet our recognition of the transformative power of shared value is still in its genesis. Realizing it will require leaders and managers to develop new skills and knowledge—such as a far deeper appreciation of societal needs, a greater understanding of the true bases of company productivity, and the ability to collaborate across profit/nonprofit boundaries. And government must learn how to regulate in ways that enable shared value rather than work against it.

Creating Shared Value

Capitalism is an unparalleled vehicle for meeting human needs, improving efficiency, creating jobs, and building wealth. But a narrow conception of apitalism has prevented business from harnessing its full potential to meet society's broader challenges. The opportunities have been there all along but have been overlooked. Businesses acting as businesses, not as charitable donors, are the most powerful force for addressing the pressing issues we face. The moment for a new conception of capitalism is now; society's needs are large and growing, while customers, employees, and a new generation of young people are asking business to step up.

The purpose of the corporation must be redefined as creating shared value, not just profit per se. This will drive the next wave of innovation and productivity growth in the global economy. It will also reshape capitalism and its relationship to society. Perhaps most important of all, learning how to create shared value is our best chance to legitimize business again.

Moving Beyond Trade-Offs

Business and society have been pitted against each other for too long. That is in part because economists have legitimized the idea that to provide societal benefits, companies must temper their economic success. In neoclassical thinking, a requirement for social improvement—such as safety or hiring the disabled—imposes a constraint on the corporation. Adding a constraint to a firm that is already maximizing profits, says the theory, will inevitably raise costs and reduce those profits.

A related concept, with the same conclusion, is the notion of externalities. Externalities arise when firms create social costs that they do not have to bear, such as pollution. Thus, society must impose taxes, regulations, and penalties so that firms "internalize" these externalities— a belief influencing many government policy decisions.

This perspective has also shaped the strategies of firms themselves, which have largely excluded social and environmental considerations from their economic thinking. Firms have taken the broader context in which they do business as a given and resisted regulatory standards as invariably contrary to their interests. Solving social problems has been ceded to governments and to NGOs. Corporate responsibility programs—a reaction to external pressure—have emerged largely to improve firms' reputations and are treated as a necessary expense. Anything more is seen by many as an irresponsible use of shareholders' money. Governments, for their part, have often regulated in a way that makes shared value more difficult to achieve. Implicitly, each side has assumed that the other is an obstacle to pursuing its goals and acted accordingly.

The concept of shared value, in contrast, recognizes that societal needs, not just conventional economic needs, define markets. It also recognizes that social harms or weaknesses frequently create *internal* costs for firms—such as wasted energy or raw materials, costly accidents, and the need for remedial training to compensate for inadequacies in education. And addressing societal harms and constraints does not necessarily raise costs for firms, because they can innovate through using new technologies, operating methods, and management approaches—and as a result, increase their productivity and expand their markets.

Shared value, then, is not about personal values. Nor is it about "sharing" the value already created by firms—a redistribution approach. Instead, it is about expanding the total pool of economic and social value. A good example of this difference in perspective is the fair trade movement in purchasing. Fair trade aims to increase the proportion of revenue that goes to poor farmers by paying them higher prices for the same crops. Though this may be a noble sentiment, fair trade is mostly about redistribution rather than expanding the overall amount of value created. A shared value perspective, instead, focuses on improving growing techniques and strengthening the local cluster of supporting suppliers and other institutions in order to increase farmers' efficiency, yields, product quality, and sustainability. This leads to a bigger pie of revenue and profits that benefits both farmers and the companies that buy from them. Early studies of cocoa farmers in the Côte d'Ivoire, for instance, suggest that while fair trade can increase farmers' incomes by 10% to 20%, shared value investments can raise their incomes by more than 300%. Initial investment and time may be required to implement new procurement practices and develop the supporting cluster, but the return will be greater economic value and broader strategic benefits for all participants.

The Roots of Shared Value

At a very basic level, the competitiveness of a company and the health of the communities around it are closely intertwined. A business needs a successful community, not only to create demand for its products but also to provide critical public assets and a supportive environment. A community needs successful businesses to provide jobs and wealth creation opportunities for its citizens. This interdependence means that public policies that undermine the productivity and competitiveness of businesses are self-defeating, especially in a global economy where facilities and jobs can easily move elsewhere. NGOs and governments have not always appreciated this connection.

In the old, narrow view of capitalism, business contributes to society by making a profit, which supports employment, wages, purchases, investments, and taxes. Conducting business as usual is sufficient social benefit. A firm is largely a self-contained entity, and social or community issues fall outside its proper scope. (This is the argument advanced persuasively by Milton Friedman in his critique of the whole notion of corporate social responsibility.)

This perspective has permeated management thinking for the past two decades. Firms focused on enticing consumers to buy more and more of their products. Facing growing competition and shorterterm performance pressures from shareholders, managers resorted to waves of restructuring, personnel reductions, and relocation to lower-cost regions, while leveraging balance sheets to return capital to investors. The results were often commoditization, price competition, little true innovation, slow organic growth, and no clear competitive advantage.

In this kind of competition, the communities in which companies operate perceive little benefit even as profits rise. Instead, they perceive that profits come at their expense, an impression that has become even stronger in the current economic recovery, in which rising earnings have done little to offset high unemployment, local business distress, and severe pressures on community services.

It was not always this way. The best companies once took on a broad range of roles in meeting the needs of workers, communities, and supporting businesses. As other social institutions appeared on the scene, however, these roles fell away or were delegated. Shortening investor time horizons began to narrow thinking about appropriate investments. As the vertically integrated firm gave way to greater reliance on outside vendors, outsourcing and offshoring weakened the connection between firms and their communities. As firms moved disparate activities to more and more locations, they often lost touch with any location. Indeed, many companies no longer recognize a home—but see themselves as "global" companies.

These transformations drove major progress in economic efficiency. However, something profoundly important was lost in the process, as morefundamental opportunities for value creation were missed. The scope of strategic thinking contracted.

Strategy theory holds that to be successful, a company must create a distinctive value proposition that meets the needs of a chosen set of customers.

The firm gains competitive advantage from how it configures the value chain, or the set of activities involved in creating, producing, selling, delivering, and supporting its products or services. For decades businesspeople have studied positioning and the best ways to design activities and integrate them. However, companies have overlooked opportunities to meet fundamental societal needs and misunderstood how societal harms and weaknesses affect value chains. Our field of vision has simply been too narrow.

In understanding the business environment, managers have focused most of their attention on the industry, or the particular business in which the firm competes. This is because industry structure has a decisive impact on a firm's profitability. What has been missed, however, is the profound effect that location can have on productivity and innovation. Companies have failed to grasp the importance of the broader business environment surrounding their major operations.

How Shared Value Is Created

Companies can create economic value by creating societal value. There are three distinct ways to do this: by reconceiving products and markets, redefining productivity in the value chain, and building supportive industry clusters at the company's locations. Each of these is part of the virtuous circle of shared value; improving value in one area gives rise to opportunities in the others.

The concept of shared value resets the boundaries of capitalism. By better connecting companies' success with societal improvement, it opens up many ways to serve new needs, gain efficiency, create differentiation, and expand markets.

The ability to create shared value applies equally to advanced economies and developing countries, though the specific opportunities will differ. The opportunities will also differ markedly across industries and companies but every company has them. And their range and scope is far broader than has been recognized.

Reconceiving Products and Markets

Society's needs are huge—health, better housing, improved nutrition, help for the aging, greater financial security, less environmental damage. Arguably, they are the greatest unmet needs in the global economy. In business we have spent decades learning how to parse and manufacture demand while missing the most important demand of all. Too many companies have lost sight of that most basic of questions: Is our product good for our customers? Or for our customers' customers?

In advanced economies, demand for products and services that meet societal needs is rapidly growing. Food companies that traditionally concentrated on taste and quantity to drive more and more consumption are refocusing on the fundamental need for better nutrition. Intel and IBM are both devising ways to help utilities harness digital intelligence in order to economize on power usage. Wells Fargo has developed a line of products and tools that help customers budget, manage credit, and pay down debt. Sales of GE's Ecomagination products reached $18 billion in 2009—the size of a *Fortune* 150 company. GE now predicts that revenues of Ecomagination products will grow at twice the rate of total company revenues over the next five years.

In these and many other ways, whole new avenues for innovation open up, and shared value is created. Society's gains are even greater, because businesses will often be far more effective than governments and nonprofits are at marketing that motivates customers to embrace products and services that create societal benefits, like healthier food or environmentally friendly products.

Equal or greater opportunities arise from serving disadvantaged communities and developing countries. Though societal needs are even more pressing there, these communities have not been recognized as viable markets. Today attention is riveted on India, China, and increasingly, Brazil, which offer firms the prospect of reaching billions of new customers at the bottom of the pyramid—a notion persuasively articulated by C.K. Prahalad. Yet these countries have always had huge needs, as do many developing countries.

Similar opportunities await in nontraditional communities in advanced countries. We have learned, for example, that poor urban areas are America's most underserved market; their substantial concentrated purchasing power has often been overlooked. (See the research of the Initiative for a Competitive Inner City, at icic.org.)

The societal benefits of providing appropriate products to lower-income and disadvantaged consumers can be profound, while the profits for companies can be substantial. For example, low-priced cell phones that provide mobile banking services are helping the poor save money securely and transforming the ability of small farmers to produce and market their crops. In Kenya, Vodafone's M-PESA mobile banking service signed up 10 million customers in three years; the funds it handles now represent 11% of that country's GDP. In India, Thomson Reuters has developed a promising monthly service for farmers who earn an average of $2,000 a year. For a fee of $5 a quarter, it provides weather and croppricing information and agricultural advice. The service reaches an estimated 2 million farmers, and early research indicates that it has helped increase the incomes of more than 60% of them—in some cases even tripling incomes. As capitalism begins to work in poorer communities, new opportunities for economic development and social progress increase exponentially.

For a company, the starting point for creating this kind of shared value is to identify all the societal needs, benefits, and harms that are or could be embodied in the firm's products. The opportunities are not static; they change constantly as technology evolves, economies develop, and societal priorities shift. An ongoing exploration of societal needs will lead companies to discover new opportunities for differentiation and repositioning in traditional markets, and to recognize the potential of new markets they previously overlooked.

Meeting needs in underserved markets often requires redesigned products or different distribution methods. These requirements can trigger fundamental innovations that also have application in traditional markets. Microfinance, for example, was invented to serve unmet financing needs in developing countries. Now it is growing rapidly in the United States, where it is filling an important gap that was unrecognized.

Redefining Productivity In the Value Chain

A company's value chain inevitably affects—and is affected by—numerous societal issues, such as natural resource and water use, health and safety, working conditions, and equal treatment in the workplace. Opportunities to create shared value arise because societal problems can create economic costs in the firm's value chain. Many so-called externalities actually inflict internal costs on the firm, even in the absence of regulation or resource taxes. Excess packaging of products and greenhouse gases are not just costly to the environment but costly to the business. Wal-Mart, for example, was able to address both issues by reducing its packaging and rerouting its trucks to cut 100 million miles from its delivery routes in 2009, saving $200 million even as it shipped more products. Innovation in disposing of plastic used in stores has saved millions in lower disposal costs to landfills.

The new thinking reveals that the congruence between societal progress and productivity in the value chain is far greater than traditionally believed. The synergy increases when firms approach societal issues from a shared value perspective and invent new ways of operating to address them. So far, however, few companies have reaped the full productivity benefits in areas such as health, safety, environmental performance, and employee retention and capability.

But there are unmistakable signs of change. Efforts to minimize pollution were once thought to inevitably increase business costs and to occur only because of regulation and taxes. Today there is a growing consensus that major improvements in environmental performance can often be achieved with better technology at nominal incremental cost and can even yield net cost savings through enhanced resource utilization, process efficiency, and quality.

In each of the areas in the exhibit, a deeper understanding of productivity and a growing awareness of the fallacy of short-term cost reductions (which often actually lower productivity or make it unsustainable) are giving rise to new approaches. The following are some of the most important ways in which shared value thinking is transforming the value chain, which are not independent but often mutually reinforcing. Efforts in these and other areas are still works in process, whose implications will be felt for years to come.

Energy use and logistics. The use of energy throughout the value chain is being reexamined, whether it be in processes, transportation, buildings, supply chains, distribution channels, or support services. Triggered by energy price spikes and a new awareness of opportunities for energy efficiency, this reexamination was under way even before carbon emissions became a global focus. The result has been striking improvements in energy utilization through better technology, recycling, cogeneration, and numerous other practices—all of which create shared value.

We are learning that shipping is expensive, not just because of energy costs and emissions but because it adds time, complexity, inventory costs, and management costs. Logistical systems are beginning to be redesigned to reduce shipping distances, streamline handling, improve vehicle routing, and the like. All of these steps create shared value. The British retailer Marks & Spencer's ambitious overhaul of its supply chain, for example, which involves steps as simple as stopping the purchase of supplies from one hemisphere to ship to another, is expected to save the retailer £175 million annually by fiscal 2016, while hugely reducing carbon emissions. In the process of reexamining logistics, thinking about outsourcing and location will also be revised (as we will discuss below).

Resource use. Heightened environmental awareness and advances in technology are catalyzing new approaches in areas such as utilization of water, raw materials, and packaging, as well as expanding recycling and reuse. The opportunities apply to all resources, not just those that have been identified by environmentalists. Better resource utilization—enabled by improving technology—will permeate all parts of the value chain and will spread to suppliers and channels. Landfills will fill more slowly.

For example, Coca-Cola has already reduced its worldwide water consumption by 9% from a 2004 baseline—nearly halfway to its goal of a 20% reduction by 2012. Dow Chemical managed to reduce consumption of fresh water at its largest production site by one billion gallons—enough water to supply nearly 40,000 people in the U.S. for a year—resulting in savings of $4 million. The demand for water-saving technology has allowed India's Jain Irrigation, a leading global manufacturer of complete drip irrigation systems for water conservation, to achieve a 41% compound annual growth rate in revenue over the past five years

Procurement. The traditional playbook calls for companies to commoditize and exert maximum bargaining power on suppliers to drive down prices— even when purchasing from small businesses or subsistence-level farmers. More recently, firms have been rapidly outsourcing to suppliers in lower-wage locations.

Today some companies are beginning to understand that marginalized suppliers cannot remain productive or sustain, much less improve, their quality. By increasing access to inputs, sharing technology, and providing financing, companies can improve supplier quality and productivity while ensuring access to growing volume. Improving productivity will often trump lower prices. As suppliers get stronger, their environmental impact often falls dramatically, which further improves their efficiency. Shared value is created.

A good example of such new procurement thinking can be found at Nespresso, one of Nestlé's fastestgrowing divisions, which has enjoyed annual growth of 30% since 2000. Nespresso combines a sophisticated espresso machine with single-cup aluminum capsules containing ground coffees from around the world. Offering quality and convenience, Nespresso has expanded the market for premium coffee.

Obtaining a reliable supply of specialized coffees is extremely challenging, however. Most coffees are grown by small farmers in impoverished rural areas of Africa and Latin America, who are trapped in a cycle of low productivity, poor quality, and environmental degradation that limits production volume. To address these issues, Nestlé redesigned procurement. It worked intensively with its growers, providing advice on farming practices, guaranteeing bank loans, and helping secure inputs such as plant stock, pesticides, and fertilizers. Nestlé established local facilities to measure the quality of the coffee at the point of purchase, which allowed it to pay a premium for better beans directly to the growers and thus improve their incentives. Greater yield per hectare and higher production quality increased growers' incomes, and the environmental impact of farms shrank. Meanwhile, Nestlé's reliable supply of good coffee grew significantly. Shared value was created.

Embedded in the Nestlé example is a far broader insight, which is the advantage of buying from capable local suppliers. Outsourcing to other locations and countries creates transaction costs and inefficiencies that can offset lower wage and input costs. Capable local suppliers help firms avoid these costs and can reduce cycle time, increase flexibility, foster faster learning, and enable innovation. Buying local includes not only local companies but also local units of national or international companies. When firms buy locally, their suppliers can get stronger, increase their profits, hire more people, and pay better wages—all of which will benefit other businesses in the community. Shared value is created.

Distribution. Companies are beginning to reexamine distribution practices from a shared value perspective. As iTunes, Kindle, and Google Scholar (which offers texts of scholarly literature online) demonstrate, profitable new distribution models can also dramatically reduce paper and plastic usage. Similarly, microfinance has created a cost-efficient new model of distributing financial services to small businesses.

even greater in nontraditional markets. For example, Hindustan Unilever is creating a new directto-home distribution system, run by underprivileged female entrepreneurs, in Indian villages of fewer than 2,000 people. Unilever provides microcredit and training and now has more than 45,000 entrepreneurs covering some 100,000 villages across 15 Indian states. Project Shakti, as this distribution system is called, benefits communities not only by giving women skills that often double their household income but also by reducing the spread of communicable diseases through increased access to hygiene products. This is a good example of how the unique ability of business to market to hardto-reach consumers can benefit society by getting life-altering products into the hands of people that need them. Project Shakti now accounts for 5% of Unilever's total revenues in India and has extended the company's reach into rural areas and built its brand in media-dark regions, creating major economic value for the company.

Employee productivity. The focus on holding down wage levels, reducing benefits, and offshoring is beginning to give way to an awareness of the positive effects that a living wage, safety, wellness, training, and opportunities for advancement for employees have on productivity. Many companies, for example, traditionally sought to minimize the cost of "expensive" employee health care coverage or even eliminate health coverage altogether. Today leading companies have learned that because of lost workdays and diminished employee productivity, poor health costs them more than health benefits do. Take Johnson & Johnson. By helping employees stop smoking (a two-thirds reduction in the past 15 years) and implementing numerous other wellness programs, the company has saved $250 million on health care costs, a return of $2.71 for every dollar spent on wellness from 2002 to 2008. Moreover, Johnson & Johnson has benefited from a more present and productive workforce. If labor unions focused more on shared value, too, these kinds of employee approaches would spread even faster.

Location. Business thinking has embraced the myth that location no longer matters, because logistics are inexpensive, information flows rapidly, and markets are global. The cheaper the location, then, the better. Concern about the local communities in which a company operates has faded.

That oversimplified thinking is now being challenged, partly by the rising costs of energy and carbon emissions but also by a greater recognition of the productivity cost of highly dispersed production systems and the hidden costs of distant procurement discussed earlier. Wal-Mart, for example, is increasingly sourcing produce for its food sections from local farms near its warehouses. It has discovered that the savings on transportation costs and the ability to restock in smaller quantities more than offset the lower prices of industrial farms farther away. Nestlé is establishing smaller plants closer to its markets and stepping up efforts to maximize the use of locally available materials.

The calculus of locating activities in developing countries is also changing. Olam International, a leading cashew producer, traditionally shipped its nuts from Africa to Asia for processing at facilities staffed by productive Asian workers. But by opening local processing plants and training workers in Tanzania, Mozambique, Nigeria, and Côte d'Ivoire, Olam has cut processing and shipping costs by as much as 25%—not to mention, greatly reduced carbon emissions. In making this move, Olam also built preferred relationships with local farmers. And it has provided direct employment to 17,000 people—95% of whom are women—and indirect employment to an equal number of people, in rural areas where jobs otherwise were not available.

These trends may well lead companies to remake their value chains by moving some activities closer to home and having fewer major production locations. Until now, many companies have thought that being global meant moving production to locations with the lowest labor costs and designing their supply chains to achieve the most immediate impact on expenses. In reality, the strongest international competitors will often be those that can establish deeper roots in important communities. Companies that can embrace this new locational thinking will create shared value.

As these examples illustrate, reimagining value chains from the perspective of shared value will offer significant new ways to innovate and unlock new economic value that most businesses have missed.

Enabling Local Cluster Development

No company is self-contained. The success of every company is affected by the supporting companies and infrastructure around it. Productivity and innovation are strongly influenced by "clusters," or geographic concentrations of firms, related businesses, suppliers, service providers, and logistical infrastructure in a particular field—such as IT in Silicon Valley, cut flowers in Kenya, and diamond cutting in Surat, India.

Clusters include not only businesses but institutions such as academic programs, trade associations, and standards organizations. They also draw on the broader public assets in the surrounding community, such as schools and universities, clean water, faircompetition laws, quality standards, and market transparency.

Clusters are prominent in all successful and growing regional economies and play a crucial role in driving productivity, innovation, and competitiveness.

Capable local suppliers foster greater logistical efficiency and ease of collaboration, as we have discussed. Stronger local capabilities in such areas as training, transportation services, and related industries also boost productivity. Without a supporting cluster, conversely, productivity suffers. Deficiencies in the framework conditions surrounding the cluster also create internal costs for firms. Poor public education imposes productivity and remedial-training costs. Poor transportation infrastructure drives up the costs of logistics. Gender or racial discrimination reduces the pool of capable employees. Poverty limits the demand for products and leads to environmental degradation, unhealthy workers, and high security costs. As companies have increasingly become disconnected from their communities, however, their influence in solving these problems has waned even as their costs have grown.

Firms create shared value by building clusters to improve company productivity while addressing gaps or failures in the framework conditions surrounding the cluster. Efforts to develop or attract capable suppliers, for example, enable the procurement benefits we discussed earlier. A focus on clusters and location has been all but absent in management thinking. Cluster thinking has also been missing in many economic development initiatives, which have failed because they involved isolated interventions and overlooked critical complementary investments.

A key aspect of cluster building in developing and developed countries alike is the formation of open and transparent markets. In inefficient or monopolized markets where workers are exploited, where suppliers do not receive fair prices, and where price transparency is lacking, productivity suffers. Enabling fair and open markets, which is often best done in conjunction with partners, can allow a company to secure reliable supplies and give suppliers better incentives for quality and efficiency while also substantially improving the incomes and purchasing power of local citizens. A positive cycle of economic and social development results.

When a firm builds clusters in its key locations, it also amplifies the connection between its success and its communities' success. A firm's growth has multiplier effects, as jobs are created in supporting industries, new companies are seeded, and demand for ancillary services rises. A company's efforts to improve framework conditions for the cluster spill over to other participants and the local economy. Workforce development initiatives, for example, increase the supply of skilled employees for many other firms as well.

At Nespresso, Nestlé also worked to build clusters, which made its new procurement practices far more effective. It set out to build agricultural, technical, financial, and logistical firms and capabilities in each coffee region, to further support efficiency and high-quality local production. Nestlé led efforts to increase access to essential agricultural inputs such as plant stock, fertilizers, and irrigation equipment; strengthen regional farmer co-ops by helping them finance shared wet-milling facilities for producing higher-quality beans; and support an extension program to advise all farmers on growing techniques. It also worked in partnership with the Rainforest Alliance, a leading international NGO, to teach farmers more-sustainable practices that make production volumes more reliable. In the process, Nestlé's productivity improved.

A good example of a company working to improve framework conditions in its cluster is Yara, the world's largest mineral fertilizer company. Yara realized that the lack of logistical infrastructure in many parts of Africa was preventing farmers from gaining efficient access to fertilizers and other essential agricultural inputs, and from transporting their crops efficiently to market. Yara is tackling this problem through a $60 million investment in a program to improve ports and roads, which is designed to create agricultural growth corridors in Mozambique and Tanzania. The company is working on this initiative with local governments and support from the Norwegian government. In Mozambique alone, the corridor is expected to benefit more than 200,000 small farmers and create 350,000 new jobs. The improvements will help Yara grow its business but will support the whole agricultural cluster, creating huge multiplier effects.

The benefits of cluster building apply not only in emerging economies but also in advanced countries. North Carolina's Research Triangle is a notable example of public and private collaboration that has created shared value by developing clusters in such areas as information technology and life sciences. That region, which has benefited from continued investment from both the private sector and local government, has experienced huge growth in employment, incomes, and company performance, and has fared better than most during the downturn.

To support cluster development in the communities in which they operate, companies need to identify gaps and deficiencies in areas such as logistics, suppliers, distribution channels, training, market organization, and educational institutions. Then the task is to focus on the weaknesses that represent the greatest constraints to the company's own productivity and growth, and distinguish those areas that the company is best equipped to influence directly from those in which collaboration is more cost-effective. Here is where the shared value opportunities will be greatest. Initiatives that address cluster weaknesses that constrain companies will be much more effective than community-focused corporate social responsibility programs, which often have limited impact because they take on too many areas without focusing on value.

But efforts to enhance infrastructure and institutions in a region often require collective action, as the Nestlé, Yara, and Research Triangle examples show. Companies should try to enlist partners to share the cost, win support, and assemble the right skills. The most successful cluster development programs are ones that involve collaboration within the private sector, as well as trade associations, government agencies, and NGOs.

Creating Shared Value in Practice

Not all profit is equal—an idea that has been lost in the narrow, short-term focus of financial markets and in much management thinking. Profits involving a social purpose represent a higher form of capitalism—one that will enable society to advance more rapidly while allowing companies to grow even more. The result is a positive cycle of company and community prosperity, which leads to profits that endure.

Creating shared value presumes compliance with the law and ethical standards, as well as mitigating any harm caused by the business, but goes far beyond that. The opportunity to create economic value through creating societal value will be one of the most powerful forces driving growth in the global economy. This thinking represents a new way of understanding customers, productivity, and the exexternal influences on corporate success. It highlights the immense human needs to be met, the large new markets to serve, and the internal costs of social and community deficits—as well as the competitive advantages available from addressing them. Until recently, companies have simply not approached their businesses this way.

Creating shared value will be more effective and far more sustainable than the majority of today's corporate efforts in the social arena. Companies will make real strides on the environment, for example, when they treat it as a productivity driver rather than a feel-good response to external pressure. Or consider access to housing. A shared value approach would have led financial services companies to create innovative products that prudently increased access to home ownership. This was recognized by the Mexican construction company Urbi, which pioneered a mortgage-financing "rent-to-own" plan. Major U.S. banks, in contrast, promoted unsustainable financing vehicles that turned out to be socially and economically devastating, while claiming they were socially responsible because they had charitable contribution programs.

Inevitably, the most fertile opportunities for creating shared value will be closely related to a company's particular business, and in areas most important to the business. Here a company can benefit the most economically and hence sustain its commitment over time. Here is also where a company brings the most resources to bear, and where its scale and market presence equip it to have a meaningful impact on a societal problem.

Ironically, many of the shared value pioneers have been those with more-limited resources—social entrepreneurs and companies in developing countries. These outsiders have been able to see the opportunities more clearly. In the process, the distinction between for-profits and nonprofits is blurring.

Shared value is defining a whole new set of best practices that all companies must embrace. It will also become an integral part of strategy. The essence of strategy is choosing a unique positioning and a distinctive value chain to deliver on it. Shared value opens up many new needs to meet, new products to offer, new customers to serve, and new ways to configure the value chain. And the competitive advantages that arise from creating shared value will often be more sustainable than conventional cost and quality improvements. The cycle of imitation and zero-sum competition can be broken.

The opportunity to create shared value are widespread and growing. Not every company will have them in every area, but our experience has been that companies discover more and more opportunities over time as their line operating units grasp this concept. It has taken a decade, but GE's Ecomagination initiative, for example, is now producing a stream of fast-growing products and services across the company.

A shared value lens can be applied to every major company decision. Could our product design incorporate greater social benefits? Are we serving all the communities that would benefit from our products? Do our processes and logistical approaches maximize efficiencies in energy and water use? Could our new plant be constructed in a way that achieves greater community impact? How are gaps in our cluster holding back our efficiency and speed of innovation? How could we enhance our community as a business location? If sites are comparable economically, at which one will the local community benefit the most? If a company can improve societal conditions, it will often improve business conditions and thereby trigger positive feedback loops.

The three avenues for creating shared value are mutually reinforcing. Enhancing the cluster, for example, will enable more local procurement and less dispersed supply chains. New products and services that meet social needs or serve overlooked markets will require new value chain choices in areas such as production, marketing, and distribution. And new value chain configurations will create demand for equipment and technology that save energy, conserve resources, and support employees.

Creating shared value will require concrete and tailored metrics for each business unit in each of the three areas. While some companies have begun to track various social impacts, few have yet tied them to their economic interests at the business level.

Shared value creation will involve new and heightened forms of collaboration. While some shared value opportunities are possible for a company to seize on its own, others will benefit from insights, skills, and resources that cut across profit/ nonprofit and private/public boundaries. Here, companies will be less successful if they attempt to tackle societal problems on their own, especially those involving cluster development. Major competitors may also need to work together on precompetitive framework conditions, something that has not been common in reputation-driven CSR initiatives. Successful collaboration will be data driven, clearly linked to defined outcomes, well connected to the goals of all stakeholders, and tracked with clear metrics.

Governments and NGOs can enable and reinforce shared value or work against it. (For more on this topic, see the section "Government Regulation and Shared Value.")

The Next Evolution in Capitalism

Shared value holds the key to unlocking the next wave of business innovation and growth. It will also reconnect company success and community success in ways that have been lost in an age of narrow management approaches, short-term thinking, and deepening divides among society's institutions.

Shared value focuses companies on the right kind of profits—profits that create societal benefits rather than diminish them. Capital markets will undoubtedly continue to pressure companies to generate short-term profits, and some companies will surely continue to reap profits at the expense of societal needs. But such profits will often prove to be shortlived, and far greater opportunities will be missed.

The moment for an expanded view of value creation has come. A host of factors, such as the growing social awareness of employees and citizens and the increased scarcity of natural resources, will drive unprecedented opportunities to create shared value.

We need a more sophisticated form of capitalism, one imbued with a social purpose. But that purpose should arise not out of charity but out of a deeper understanding of competition and economic value creation. This next evolution in the capitalist model recognizes new and better ways to develop products, serve markets, and build productive enterprises.

Creating shared value represents a broader conception of Adam Smith's invisible hand. It opens the doors of the pin factory to a wider set of influences. It is not philanthropy but self-interested behavior to create economic value by creating societal value. If all companies individually pursued shared value connected to their particular businesses, society's overall interests would be served. And companies would acquire legitimacy in the eyes of the communities in which they operated, which would allow democracy to work as governments set policies that fostered and supported business. Survival of the fittest would still prevail, but market competition would benefit society in ways we have lost.

Creating shared value represents a new approach to managing that cuts across disciplines. Because of the traditional divide between economic concerns and social ones, people in the public and private sectors have often followed very different educational and career paths. As a result, few managers have the understanding of social and environmental issues required to move beyond today's CSR approaches, and few social sector leaders have the managerial training and entrepreneurial mind-set needed to design and implement shared value models. Most business schools still teach the narrow view of capitalism, even though more and more of their graduates hunger for a greater sense of purpose and a growing number are drawn to social entrepreneurship. The results have been missed opportunity and public cynicism.

Business school curricula will need to broaden in a number of areas. For example, the efficient use and stewardship of all forms of resources will define the next-generation thinking on value chains. Customer behavior and marketing courses will have to move beyond persuasion and demand creation to the study of deeper human needs and how to serve nontraditional customer groups. Clusters, and the broader locational influences on company productivity and innovation, will form a new core discipline in business schools; economic development will no longer be left only to public policy and economics departments. Business and government courses will examine the economic impact of societal factors on enterprises, moving beyond the effects of regulation and macroeconomics. And finance will need to rethink how capital markets can actually support true value creation in companies—their fundamental purpose—not just benefit financial market participants.

There is nothing soft about the concept of shared value. These proposed changes in business school curricula are not qualitative and do not depart from economic value creation. Instead, they represent the next stage in our understanding of markets, competition, and business management.

Not all societal problems can be solved through shared value solutions. But shared value offers corporations the opportunity to utilize their skills, resources, and management capability to lead social progress in ways that even the best-intentioned governmental and social sector organizations can rarely match. In the process, businesses can earn the respect of society again.

Creating Shared Value

What Is "Shared Value"?

The concept of shared value can be defined as policies and operating practices that enhance the competitiveness of a company while simultaneously advancing the economic and social conditions in the communities in which it operates. Shared value creation focuses on identifying and expanding the connections between societal and economic progress.

The concept rests on the premise that both economic and social progress must be addressed using value principles. Value is defined as benefits relative to costs, not just benefits alone. Value creation is an idea that has long been recognized in business, where profit is revenues earned from customers minus the costs incurred. However, businesses have rarely approached societal issues from a value perspective but have treated them as peripheral matters. This has obscured the connections between economic and social concerns. In the social sector, thinking in value terms is even less common.

Social organizations and government entities often see success solely in terms of the benefits achieved or the money expended. As governments and NGOs begin to think more in value terms, their interest in collaborating with business will inevitably grow.

Blurr ing the Profit/Nonprofit Boundary

The concept of shared value blurs the line between for-profit and nonprofit organizations. New kinds of hybrid enterprises are rapidly appearing. For example, WaterHealth International, a fast-growing forprofit, uses innovative water purification techniques to distribute clean water at minimal cost to more than one million people in rural India, Ghana, and the Philippines. Its investors include not only the socially focused Acumen Fund and the International Finance Corporation of the World Bank but also Dow Chemical's venture fund. Revolution Foods, a four-year-old venture-capital-backed U.S. start-up, provides 60,000 fresh, healthful, and nutritious meals to students daily—and does so at a higher gross margin than traditional competitors. Waste Concern, a hybrid profit/nonprofit enterprise started in Bangladesh 15 years ago, has built the capacity to convert 700 tons of trash, collected daily from neighborhood slums, into organic fertilizer, thereby increasing crop yields and reducing CO_2 emissions. Seeded with capital from the Lions Club and the United Nations Development Programme, the company improves health conditions while earning a substantial gross margin through fertilizer sales and carbon credits.

The blurring of the boundary between successful for-profits and nonprofits is one of the strong signs that creating shared value is possible.

The Connection Betw een Competitive Advantage and Social Issues

There are numerous ways in which addressing societal concerns can yield productivity benefits to a firm. Consider, for example, what happens when a firm invests in a wellness program.

Society benefits because employees and their families become healthier, and the firm minimizes employee absences and lost productivity. The graphic below depicts some areas where the connections are strongest.

The Role of Social Entrepreneurs

Businesses are not the only players in finding profitable solutions to social problems. A whole generation of social entrepreneurs is pioneering new product concepts that meet social needs using viable business models. Because they are not locked into narrow traditional business thinking, social entrepreneurs are often well ahead of established corporations in discovering these opportunities. Social enterprises that create shared value can scale up far more rapidly than purely social programs, which often suffer from an inability to grow and become self-sustaining. Real social entrepreneurship should be measured by its ability to create shared value, not just social benefit.

Implications for Government and Civil Society *While our focus here is primarily on companies, the principles of shared value apply equally to governments and nonprofit organizations.*

Governments and NGOs will be most effective if they think in value terms—considering benefits relative to costs—and focus on the results achieved rather than the funds and effort expended. Activists have tended to approach social improvement from an ideological or absolutist perspective, as if social benefits should be pursued at any cost. Governments and NGOs often assume that trade-offs between economic and social benefits are inevitable, exacerbating these trade-offs through their approaches. For example, much environmental regulation still takes the form of command-and-control mandates and enforcement actions designed to embarrass and punish companies. Regulators would accomplish much more by focusing on measuring environmental performance and introducing standards, phase-in periods, and support for technology that would promote innovation, improve the environment, and increase competitiveness simultaneously.

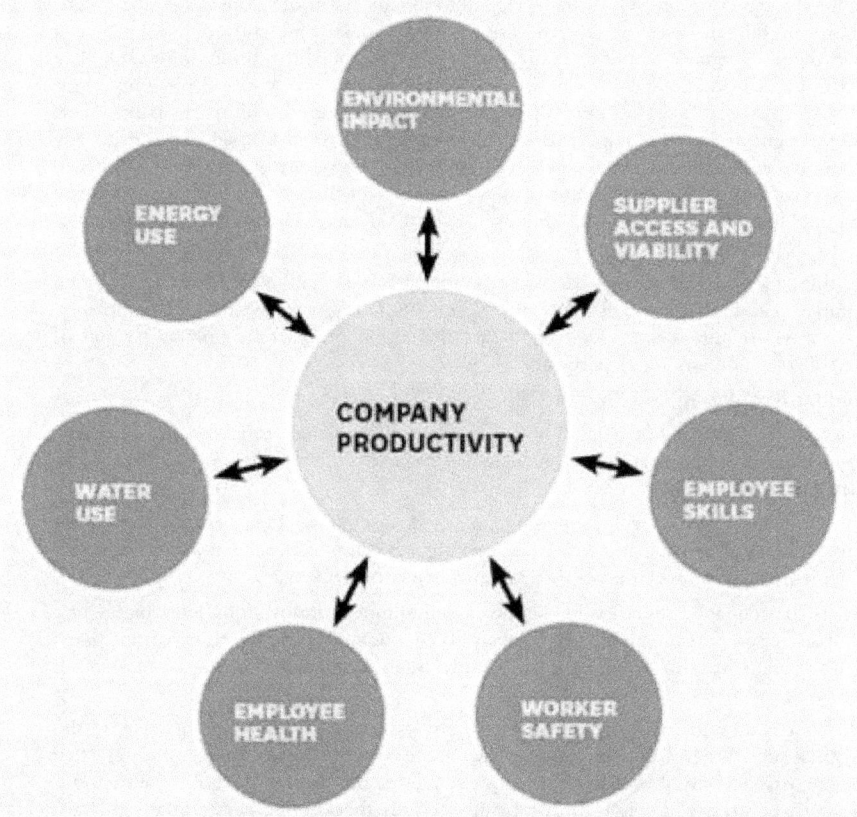

The principle of shared value creation cuts across the traditional divide between the responsibilities of business and those of government or civil society. From society's perspective, it does not matter what types of organizations created the value. What matters is that benefits are delivered by those organizations—or combinations of organizations—that are best positioned to achieve the most impact for the least cost. Finding ways to boost productivity is equally valuable whether in the service of commercial or societal objectives. In short, the principle of value creation should guide the use of resources across all areas of societal concern.

Fortunately, a new type of NGO has emerged that understands the importance of productivity and value creation. Such organizations have often had a remarkable impact. One example is TechnoServe, which has partnered with both regional and global corporations to promote the development of competitive agricultural clusters in more than 30 countries. Root Capital accomplishes a similar objective by providing financing to farmers and businesses that are too large for microfinance but too small for normal bank financing. Since 2000, Root Capital has lent more than $200 million to 282 businesses, through which it has reached 400,000 farmers and artisans. It has financed the cultivation of 1.4 million acres of organic agriculture in Latin America and Africa. Root Capital regularly works with corporations, utilizing future purchase orders as collateral for its loans to farmers and helping to strengthen corporate supply chains and improve the quality of purchased inputs.

Some private foundations have begun to see the power of working with businesses to create shared value. The Bill & Melinda Gates Foundation, for example, has formed partnerships with leading global corporations to foster agricultural clusters in developing countries. The foundation carefully focuses on commodities where climate and soil conditions give a particular region a true competitive advantage. The partnerships bring in NGOs like TechnoServe and Root Capital, as well as government officials, to work on precompetitive issues that improve the cluster and upgrade the value chain for all participants. This approach recognizes that helping small farmers increase their yields will not create any lasting benefits unless there are ready buyers for their crops, other enterprises that can process the crops once they are harvested, and a local cluster that includes efficient logistical infrastructure, input availability, and the like. The active engagement of corporations is essential to mobilizing these elements.

Forward-thinking foundations can also serve as honest brokers and allay fears by mitigating power imbalances between small local enterprises, NGOs, governments, and companies. Such efforts will require a new assumption that shared value can come only as a result of effective collaboration among all parties.

Government Regulation and Shared Value

The right kind of government regulation can encourage companies to pursue shared value; the wrong kind works against it and even makes tradeoffs between economic and social goals inevitable.

Regulation is necessary for well-functioning markets, something that became abundantly clear during the recent financial crisis. However, the ways in which regulations are designed and implemented determine whether they benefit society or work against it.

Regulations that enhance shared value set goals and stimulate innovation. They highlight a societal objective and create a level playing field to encourage companies to invest in shared value rather than maximize short-term profit. Such regulations have a number of characteristics:

First, they set clear and measurable social goals, whether they involve energy use, health matters, or safety. Where appropriate, they set prices for resources (such as water) that reflect true costs. Second, they set performance standards but do not prescribe the methods to achieve them—those are left to companies. Third, they define phase-in periods for meeting standards, which reflect the investment or new-product cycle in the industry. Phasein periods give companies time to develop and introduce new products and processes in a way consistent with the economics of their business. Fourth, they put in place universal measurement and performancereporting systems, with government investing in infrastructure for collecting reliable benchmarking data (such as nutritional deficiencies in each community). This motivates and enables continual improvement beyond current targets. Finally, appropriate regulations require efficient and timely reporting of results, which can then be audited by the government as necessary, rather than impose detailed and expensive compliance processes on everyone.

Regulation that discourages shared value looks very different. It forces compliance with particular practices, rather than focusing on measurable social improvement. It mandates a particular approach to meeting a standard—blocking innovation and almost always inflicting cost on companies. When governments fall into the trap of this sort of regulation, they undermine the very progress that they seek while triggering fierce resistance from business that slows progress further and blocks shared value that would improve cmpetitiveness.

To be sure, companies locked into the old mind-set will resist even wellconstructed regulation. As shared value principles become more widely accepted, however, business and government will become more aligned on regulation in many areas. Companies will come to understand that the right kind of regulation can actually foster economic value creation."

Finally, regulation will be needed to limit the pursuit of exploitative, unfair, or deceptive practices in which companies benefit at the expense of society. Strict antitrust policy, for example, is essential to ensure that the benefits of company success flow to customers, suppliers, and workers.

HOW SHARED VALUE DIFFERS FROM CORPORATE SOCIAL RESPONSIBILITY

Creating shared value (CSV) should supersede corporate social responsibility (CSR) in guiding the investments of companies in their communities. CSR programs focus mostly on reputation and have only a limited connection to the business, making them hard to justify and maintain over the long run. In contrast, CSV is integral to a company's profitability and competitive position. It leverages the unique resources and expertise of the company to create economic value by creating social value.

CSR → CSV

› Values: doing good	› Value: economic and societal benefits relative to cost
› Citizenship, philanthropy, sustainability	› Joint company and community value creation
› Discretionary or in response to external pressure	› Integral to competing
› Separate from profit maximization	› Integral to profit maximization
› Agenda is determined by external reporting and personal preferences	› Agenda is company specific and internally generated
› Impact limited by corporate footprint and CSR budget	› Realigns the entire company budget
Example: Fair trade purchasing	Example: Transforming procurement to increase quality and yield

In both cases, compliance with laws and ethical standards and reducing harm from corporate activities are assumed.

The Idea in Brief

The concept of shared value—which focuses on the connections between societal and economic progress—has the power to unleash the next wave of global growth.

An increasing number of companies known for their hard-nosed approach to business—such as Google, IBM, Intel, Johnson & Johnson, Nestlé, Unilever, and Wal-Mart—have begun to embark on important shared value initiatives. But our understanding of the potential of shared value is just beginning.

There are three key ways that companies can create shared value opportunities:

- By reconceiving products and markets
- By redefining productivity in the value chain
- By enabling local cluster development

Every firm should look at decisions and opportunities through the lens of shared value. This will lead to new approaches that generate greater innovation and growth for companies—and also greater benefits for society.

———————————————————————

CHAPTER 9
Managing Unpredictable Supply-Chain Disruptions

Traditional methods for managing supply chain risk rely on knowing the likelihood of occurrence and the magnitude of impact for every potential event that could materially disrupt a firm's operations. For common supply-chain disruptions—poor supplier performance, forecast errors, transportation breakdowns, and so on those methods work very well, using historical data to quantify the level of risk.

But it's a different story for low-probability, high-impact events—megadisasters like Hurricane Katrina in 2005, viral epidemics like the 2003 SARS outbreak, or major outages due to unforeseen events such as factory fires and political upheavals. Because historical data on these rare events are limited or nonexistent, their risk is hard to quantify using traditional models. As a result, many companies do not adequately prepare for them. That can have calamitous consequences when catastrophes do strike and can force even operationally savvy companies to scramble after the fact—think of Toyota following the 2011 Fukushima earthquake and tsunami.

To address this challenge, we developed a model—a mathematical description of the supply chain that can be computerized—that focuses on the impact of potential failures at points along the supply chain (such as the shuttering of a supplier's factory or a flood at a distribution center), rather than the cause of the disruption. This type of analysis obviates the need to determine the probability that any specific risk will occur—a valid approach since the mitigation strategies for a disruption are equally effective regardless of what caused it. Using the model, companies can quantify what the financial and operational impact would be if a critical supplier's facility were out of commission for, say, two weeks—whatever the reason. The computerized model can be updated easily and quickly, which is crucial since supply chains are in a continual state of flux.

In developing and applying our model at Ford Motor Company and other firms, we were surprised to find little correlation between how much a firm spends annually on procurement at a particular site and the impact that the site's disruption would have on company performance. Indeed, as the Ford case study described later in this article shows, the greatest exposures often lie in unlikely places.

In practice, that means that leaders using traditional risk-management techniques and simple heuristics (dollar amount spent at a site, for instance) often end up focusing exclusively on the so-called strategic suppliers for whom expenditures are very high and whose parts are deemed crucial to product differentiation, and overlooking the risks associated with low-cost, commodity suppliers. As a result, managers take the wrong actions, waste resources, and leave the organization exposed to hidden risk. In this article, we describe our model and how companies can use it to identify, manage, and reduce their exposure to supply chain risks.

Time to Recovery and the Risk Exposure Index

A central feature of our model is time to recovery (TTR): the time it would take for a particular node (such as a supplier facility, a distribution center, or a transportation hub) to be restored to full functionality after a disruption. TTR values are determined by examining historical experience and surveying the firm's buyers or suppliers (see the section "Assessing

Impact? Use a Simple Questionnaire"). These values can be unique for every node or can differ across a subset of the nodes.

Our model integrates TTR data with information on multiple tiers of supplier relationships, bill-of-material information, operational and financial measures, in-transit and on-site inventory levels, and demand forecasts for each product. Firms can represent their entire supply network at any level of detail—from individual parts to aggregations based on part category, supplier, geography, or product line. This allows managers to drill down into greater detail as needed and identify previously unrecognized dependencies. The model can account for disruptions of varying severity by running scenarios using TTRs of different durations.

To conduct the analysis, the model removes one node at a time from the supply network for the duration of the TTR. It then determines the supply chain response that would minimize the performance impact of the disruption at that node—for instance, drawing down inventory, shifting production, expediting transportation, or reallocating resources. On the basis of the optimal response, it generates a financial or operational performance impact (PI) for the node. A company can choose different measures of PI: lost units of production, revenue, or profit margin, for instance. The model analyzes all nodes in the network, assigning a PI to each. The node with the largest PI (in lost sales, for instance, or lost units of production) is assigned a risk exposure index (REI) score of 1.0. All other nodes' REI scores are indexed relative to this value (a node whose disruption would cause the least impact receives a value close to zero). The indexed scores allow the firm to identify at a glance the nodes that should get the most attention from risk managers.

At its core, the model uses a common mathematical technique—linear optimization to determine the best response to a node's being disrupted for the duration of its TTR. The model accounts for existing and alternative sources of supply, transportation, inventory of finished goods, work in progress and raw material, and production dependencies within the supply chain.

Our approach provides a number of benefits. It:

Identifies hidden exposures. The model helps managers identify which nodes in the network create the greatest risk exposure—often highlighting previously hidden or overlooked areas of high risk. It also allows the firm to compare the costs and benefits of various alternatives for mitigating impact.

Avoids the need for predictions about rare events. The model determines the optimal response to any disruption that might occur within the supply network, regardless of the cause. Rather than trying to quantify the likelihood that a low-probability, high-risk event will strike, firms can focus on identifying the most important exposures and putting in place risk-management strategies to mitigate them.

Reveals supply chain dependencies and bottlenecks. Companies can also use the analyses to make inventory and sourcing decisions that increase the robustness of the network. This includes taking into account the likely scramble among rival companies to lock in alternative sources if a supplier's disruption affects several firms. Such cross-firm effects of a crisis are often overlooked. Contracts with backup suppliers can be negotiated to give a company priority over others should a disruption with the primary supplier occur, which would decrease time to recovery and financial impact.

Promotes discussion and learning. In the course of analyzing the supply chain in this way, managers engage in discussions with suppliers and internal groups about acceptable levels of TTR for critical facilities and share insights about best-practice processes to reduce recovery time. As a result, the impact of disruptions is minimized.

Prescriptive Actions. Our model provides organizations with a quantitative metric for segmenting suppliers by risk level. Using data generated by the model, we can categorize suppliers along two dimensions: the total amount of money that the company spends at each supplier site in a given year, and the performance impact on the firm associated with a disruption of each supplier node. Let's now take a look at the supplier segments and consider the risk-management strategies appropriate for each.

Obvious high risk. Most companies focus their risk-management activities on suppliers for whom total spend and performance impact are both high. Typically, these are the suppliers of expensive components, such as car seats and instrument panels, that strongly affect customers' purchase decisions and experience. The cost of these "strategic components," as they're frequently called, often make up a large portion of the total manufacturing cost. Indeed, for many companies, they represent 20% of the suppliers but account for about 80% of a firm's total procurement expenditures. Because strategic components typically come from a single supplier, appropriate risk-mitigation strategies include strategic partnering with the suppliers to analyze and reduce their risk exposure, providing incentives to some suppliers to have multiple manufacturing sites in different regions, tracking suppliers' performance, and developing and implementing business continuity plans.

Low risk. Suppliers with low total spend and low financial impact do not require intense risk-management investment. In our experience, most companies effectively manage the minimal risks from disruptions of these supplier sites by investing in excess inventory or negotiating long-term contracts with a penalty clause for nonperformance.

Hidden risk. Many companies, however, are subject to considerable exposure from "hidden risk" suppliers. Here, total spend is low but the financial impact of a disruption is high. Even the savviest managers are prone to equating total spend with performance impact: They rightly identify strategic components as carrying high levels of supply chain risk, but fail to consider that low-spend suppliers, often of commodity goods, may represent outsize risks. Traditional risk-assessment exercises overlook these components because they are perceived as adding little value to the firm's products. But the reality is that markets for commodity goods are typically dominated by only a few manufacturers, leaving purchasers susceptible to disruptions. For example, in the automotive industry, a carmaker's total spend on suppliers of O-rings or valves is typically quite low, but if the supply is disrupted, the carmaker will have to shut down the production line. Thus, it is critical to ensure that an adequate supply is available. That can often be accomplished using the strategies that apply to the other segments: investing in excess inventory, requiring suppliers to operate multiple production sites, or implementing dual-sourcing strategies.

Alternatively, companies can use flexibility to deal with hidden supply risks. For example, system flexibility (the ability to quickly change the production mix of plants) allowed Pepsi Bottling Group to rapidly respond to a supply disruption caused by a fire at a chemical plant near one of its suppliers. Similarly, product-design flexibility (in this case, the use of standardized components) enabled Nokia to recover quickly from a disruption of its supply of radio frequency chips caused by a fire at a supplier's factory. Finally, process flexibility (achieved in this case by adjusting workforce skills and processes) allowed Toyota to quickly restore the supply of brake-fluid-proportioning valves (P-valves) after a major disruption.

Case Study: Ford Motor Company

We used our methodology to analyze Ford's exposure to supply chain disruptions. Working together with Keith W. Combs, Steve J. Faraci, Oleg Y. Gusikhin, and Don X. Zhang, managers in Ford's purchasing and R&D groups, we looked at two scenarios: In the first, the supplier's production facility is disrupted for two weeks. In the second, the supplier's tooling must be replaced, halting operations at its facility for eight weeks. (Details have been altered to mask sensitive Ford data.)

Ford has a multitier supplier network with long lead times from some suppliers, a complex bill-of-materials structure, buffer inventory, and components that are shared across multiple product lines. Approximately 61% of the supplier sites would have no impact on Ford's profits if they were disrupted. By contrast, about 2% of the supplier sites would, if disrupted, have a significant impact on Ford's profits. The supplier sites whose disruption would cause the greatest damage are those from which Ford's annual purchases are relatively small—a finding that surprised Ford managers. Indeed, many of those suppliers had not previously been identified by the company's risk managers as high-exposure suppliers.

Using the model, Ford was able to identify the supplier sites that required no special risk-management attention (those with short TTR and low financial impact) and those that warranted more-thorough disruption-mitigation plans. The results from the analysis allowed Ford to evaluate alternative steps it might take to defuse high-impact risks and to better prioritize its risk mitigation strategies. For example, managers learned that the risk-exposure-index scores associated with certain suppliers are highly sensitive to the amount of inventory the firm carries. For that reason, Ford put processes in place to monitor the inventory related to those suppliers on a daily basis.

In March 2012, the auto industry was rocked by a shortage of a specialty resin called nylon 12, used in the manufacture of fuel tanks, brake components, and seat fabrics. The key supplier, Evonik, had experienced a devastating explosion in its plant in Marl, Germany. It took Evonik six months to restart production, during which time the downstream production facilities of Ford and other major automakers were severely disrupted. Had Ford managers used our framework prior to this disruption, they would have detected the risk exposure and associated production bottleneck and proactively worked with Evonik to fast-track its plans to bring online a new plant in Singapore, currently slated to begin production in 2015.

Ford's supply chain, like those of many other companies, has become increasingly globalized, complex, and extended. This has had the effect of introducing more potential points of failure that Ford must recognize and manage. Using our model, it can rapidly quantify its supply chain exposure and identify effective strategies to mitigate the impact should disruptions occur.

OUR APPROACH to managing supply chain risks allows managers to avoid guessing the likelihood of infrequent, high-impact events and instead concentrate on evaluating their organization's vulnerability to disruptions, regardless of their cause and where they strike. The method is quantitative, produces a risk exposure measure that is easy to understand, and supports a supplier segmentation process that results in supply networks that are much more resilient.

Impact of Supplier Disruptions on Ford's Profits

The sites whose disruption would cause the greatest damage are those from which Ford's annual purchases are relatively small. Ford had not previously identified many of them as high-exposure suppliers. (Data have been disguised to protect sensitive competitive information.)

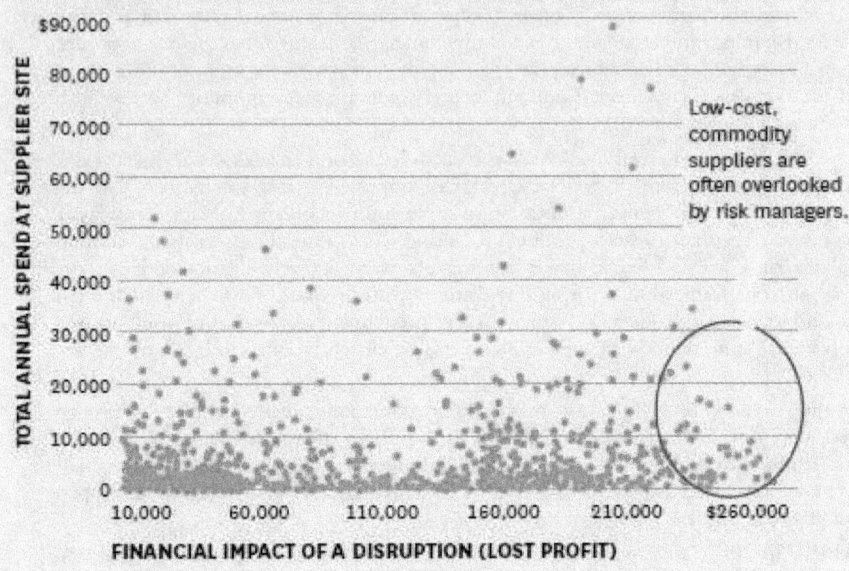

Impact of Supplier Disruptions on Ford's Profits

The sites whose disruption would cause the greatest damage are those from which Ford's annual purchases are relatively small. Ford had not previously identified many of them as high-exposure suppliers. (Data have been disguised to protect sensitive competitive information.)

TOTAL ANNUAL SPEND AT SUPPLIER SITE

Low-cost, commodity suppliers are often overlooked by risk managers.

FINANCIAL IMPACT OF A DISRUPTION (LOST PROFIT)

A High-Tech Manufacturer's Risk Exposure Index

Our model allows companies in any industry to effectively identify areas of hidden risk in the supply chain. Imagine a high-tech manufacturer that has suppliers and assembly plants all over the world. For each node in the supply chain, managers estimate the time to recovery if a disruption occurred at that node (how long it would take for the node to be restored to full operation) and then calculate the performance impact (lost sales during TTR, for instance). By indexing the performance impact values, managers can see at a glance which nodes represent the highest risks and direct their mitigation strategies accordingly.

Assessing Impact? Use a Simple Questionnaire

1 SUPPLIER

- Site location (city, region, country)

2 PARTS FROM THIS SITE

- Part number and description
- Part cost
- Annual volume for this part

- Inventory information (days of supply) for this part
- Total spend (per year) from this site

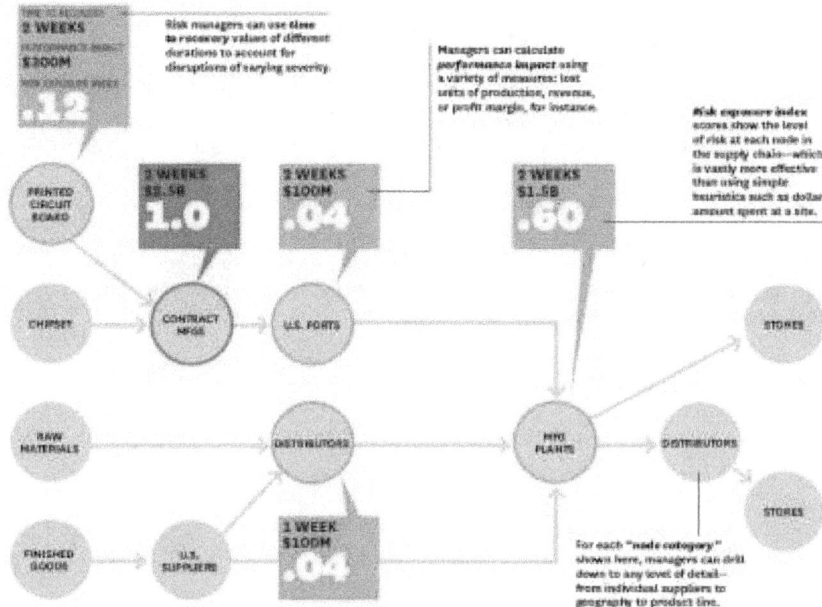

3 END PRODUCT

- OEM's end product(s) that uses this part
- Profit margin for the end product(s)

4 LEAD TIMES FROM SUPPLIER SITE TO OEM SITES

- Days

5 TIME TO RECOVERY (TTR)

The time it would take for the site to be restored to full functionality • if the supplier site is down, but the tooling is not damaged

- if the tooling is lost

6 COST OF LOSS

- Is expediting components from other locations possible? If so, what is the cost?
- Can additional resources (overtime, more shifts, alternate capacity) be organized to satisfy demand? If so, what is the cost?

7 SUPPLIER RISK ASSESSMENT

- Does the supplier produce only from a single source?
- Could alternate vendors supply the part?
- Is the supplier financially stable?
- Is there variability in performance (lead time, fill rate, quality)?

8 MITIGATION STRATEGIES FOR THIS SUPPLIER-PART COMBINATION

- Alternate suppliers
- Excess inventory
- Other

The Idea in Brief

THE PROBLEM. Traditional tools for analyzing supply chain risks require assessments of whether something is likely to happen, and the magnitude of its impact.

WHY THIS HAPPENS. A large class of risks—such as tsunamis, pandemics, and strikes—can't be assessed in this way.

THE SOLUTION. The authors have developed a model for determining the impact that a disruption of each node in its supply chain would have, regardless of its cause or likelihood. It uncovers risks that other models don't, including dangers posed by suppliers of low-cost commodities and the lack of correlation between the impact of a site disruption and dollar amount that the firm spends at that site.

CHAPTER 10
Talent Management in Challenging Environment

Every talent management process in use today was developed half a century ago It's time for a new model. by Peter Cappelli

Failures in talent management are an ongoing source of pain for executives in modern organizations. Over the past generation, talent management practices, especially in the United States, have by and large been dysfunctional, leading corporations to lurch from surpluses of talent to shortfalls to surpluses and back again.

At its heart, talent management is simply a matter of anticipating the need for human capital and then setting out a plan to meet it. Current responses to this challenge largely fall into two distinct—and equally ineffective—camps. The first, and by far the most common, is to do nothing: anticipate no needs at all; make no plans for addressing them (rendering the term "talent management" meaningless). This reactive approach relies overwhelmingly on outside hiring and has faltered now that the surplus of management talent has eroded. The second, common only among large, older companies, relies on complex and bureaucratic models from the 1950s for forecasting and succession planning legacy systems that grew up in an era when business was highly predictable and that fail now because they are inaccurate and costly in a more volatile environment.

It's time for a fundamentally new approach to talent management that takes into account the great uncertainty businesses face today. Fortunately, companies already have such a model, one that has been well honed over decades to anticipate and meet demand in uncertain environments—supply chain management. By borrowing lessons from operations and supply chain research, firms can forge a new model of talent management better suited to today's realities. Before getting into the details, let's look at the context in which talent management has evolved over the past few decades and its current state.

How We Got Here

Internal development was the norm back in the 1950s, and every management development practice that seems novel today was commonplace in those years—from executive coaching to 360-degree feedback to job rotation to high-potential programs.

Except at a few very large firms, internal talent development collapsed in the 1970s because it could not address the increasing uncertainties of the marketplace. Business forecasting had failed to predict the economic downturn in that decade, and talent pipelines continued to churn under outdated assumptions of growth. The excess supply of managers, combined with no-layoff policies for white-collar workers, fed corporate bloat. The steep recession of the early 1980s then led to white-collar layoffs and the demise of lifetime employment, as restructuring cut layers of hierarchy and eliminated many practices and staffs that developed talent. After all, if the priority was to cut positions, particularly in middle management, why maintain the programs designed to fill the ranks?

The older companies like PepsiCo and GE that still invested in development became known as "academy companies": breeding grounds for talent simply by maintaining some of the practices that nearly all corporations had followed in the past. A number of such companies managed to ride out the restructurings of the 1980s with their programs intact only to succumb to cost-cutting pressures later on.

Talent Management in Challenging Environment

The problems faced by Unilever's Indian operations after 2000 are a case in point. Known as a model employer and talent developer since the 1950s, the organization suddenly found itself top-heavy and stuck when business declined after the 2001 recession. Its well-oiled pipeline saddled the company with 1,400 well-trained managers in 2004, up 27% from 2000, despite the fact that the demand for managers had fallen. Unilever's implicit promise to avoid layoffs meant the company had to find places for them in its other international operations or buy them out.

The alternative to traditional development, outside hiring, worked like a charm through the early 1990s, in large measure because organizations were drawing on the big pool of laid-off talent. As the economy continued to grow, however, companies increasingly recruited talent away from their competitors, creating retention problems. Watching the fruits of their labors walk out the door, employers backed even further away from investments in development. I remember a conversation with a CEO in the medical device industry about a management development program proposed by his head of human resources. The CEO dismissed the proposal by saying, "Why should we develop people when our competitors are willing to do it for us?" By the mid-1990s, virtually every major corporation asserted the goal of getting better at recruiting talent away from competitors while also getting better at retaining its own talent—a hopeful dream at the individual level, an impossibility in the aggregate.

Outside hiring hit its inevitable limit by the end of the 1990s, after the longest economic expansion in U.S. history absorbed the supply of available talent. Companies found they were attracting experienced candidates and losing experienced employees to competitors at the same rate. Outside searches became increasingly expensive, particularly when they involved headhunters, and the newcomers blocked prospects for internal promotions, aggravating retention problems. The challenge of attracting and retaining the right people went to the very top of the list of executives' business concerns, where it remains today.

The good news is that most companies are facing the challenge with a pretty clean slate: Little in the way of talent management is actually going on in them. One recent study, for example, reports that two-thirds of U.S. employers are doing no workforce planning of any kind. The bad news is that the advice companies are getting is to return to the practices of the 1950s and create long-term succession plans that attempt to map out careers years into the future—even though the stable business environment and talent pipelines in which such practices were born no longer exist.

That simply won't work. Traditional approaches to succession planning assume a multiyear development process, yet during that period, strategies, org charts, and management teams will certainly change, and the groomed successors may well leave anyway. When an important vacancy occurs, it's not unusual for companies to conclude that the candidates identified by the succession plan no longer meet the needs of the job, and they look outside. Such an outcome is worse in several ways than having no plan. First, the candidates feel betrayed—succession plans create an implicit promise. Second, investments in developing these candidates are essentially wasted. Third, most companies now have to update their succession plans every year as jobs change and individuals leave, wasting tremendous amounts of time and energy. As a practical matter, how useful is a "plan" if it has to be changed every year?

Talent management is not an end in itself. It is not about developing employees or creating succession plans, nor is it about achieving specific turnover rates or any other tactical outcome. It exists to support the organization's overall objectives, which in business essentially amount to making money. Making money requires an understanding of the costs as well as the benefits associated with talent management choices. The costs inherent to the organization-man development model were largely irrelevant in the 1950s because, in an era of lifetime employment and a culture in which job-hopping was considered a sign of failure, companies that did not develop talent in-house would not have any at all. Development practices, such as rotational job assignments, were so deeply embedded that their costs were rarely questioned (though internal accounting systems were so poor that it would have been difficult to assess the costs in any case).

That's no longer true. Today's rapid-fire changes in customers' demands and competitors' offerings, executive turnover that can easily run to 10%, and increased pressure to show a financial return for every set of business practices make the develop-from-within approach too slow and risky. And yet the hire-from-without models are too expensive and disruptive to the organization.

A New Way to Think About Talent Management

Unlike talent development, models of supply chain management have improved radically since the 1950s. No longer do companies own huge warehouses where they stockpile the components needed to assemble years' worth of products they can sell with confidence because competition is muted and demand eminently predictable. Since the 1980s, companies have instituted, and continually refined, justin- time manufacturing processes and other supply chain innovations that allow them to anticipate shifts in demand and adapt products ever more accurately and quickly. What I am proposing is something akin to just-in-time manufacturing for the development realm: a talent-on-demand framework. If you consider for a moment, you will see how suited this model might be to talent development.

Forecasting product demand is comparable to forecasting talent needs; estimating the cheapest and fastest ways to manufacture products is the equivalent of cost-effectively developing talent; outsourcing certain aspects of manufacturing processes is like hiring outside; ensuring timely delivery relates to planning for succession events. The issues and challenges in managing an internal talent pipeline—how employees advance through development jobs and experiences—are remarkably similar to how products move through a supply chain: reducing bottlenecks that block advancement, speeding up processing time, improving forecasts to avoid mismatches.

The most innovative approaches to managing talent use four particular principles drawn from operations and supply chain management. Two of them address uncertainty on the demand side: how to balance make-versusbuy decisions and how to reduce the risks in forecasting the demand for talent. The other two address uncertainty on the supply side: how to improve the return on investment in development efforts and how to protect that investment by generating internal opportunities that encourage newly trained managers to stick with the firm.

Principle 1: Make *and* Buy to Manage Risk

Just as a lack of parts was the major concern of midcentury manufacturers, a shortfall of talent was the greatest concern of traditional management development systems of the 1950s and 1960s, when all leaders had to be homegrown. If a company did not produce enough skilled project managers, it had to push inexperienced people into new roles or give up on projects and forgo their revenue. Though forecasting was easier than it is today, it wasn't perfect, so the only way to avoid a shortfall was to deliberately overshoot talent demand projections. If the process produced an excess of talent, it was relatively easy to park people on a bench, just as one might put spare parts in a warehouse, until opportunities became available. It may sound absurd to suggest that an organization would maintain the equivalent of a human-capital supply closet, but that was extremely common in the organization-man period.

Today, a deep bench of talent has become expensive inventory. What's more, it's inventory that can walk out the door. Ambitious executives don't want to, and don't have to, sit on the bench. Worse, studies by the consulting firm Watson Wyatt show that people who have recently received training are the most likely to decamp, as they leave for opportunities to make better use of those new skills.

Talent Management in Challenging Environment

It still makes sense to develop talent internally where we can because it is cheaper and less disruptive. But outside hiring can be faster and more responsive. So an optimal approach would be to use a combination of the two. The challenge is to figure out how much of each to use.

To begin, we should give up on the idea that we can predict talent demand with certainty and instead own up to the fact that our forecasts, especially the long-range ones, will almost never be perfect. With the error rate on a one-year forecast of demand for an individual product hovering around 33%, and with nonstop organizational restructurings and changes in corporate strategy, the idea that we can accurately predict talent demand for an entire company several years out is a myth. Leading corporations like Capital One and Dow Chemical have abandoned longterm talent forecasts and moved toward shortterm simulations: Operating executives give talent planners their best guess as to what business demands will be over the next few years; the planners use sophisticated simulation software to tell them what that will require in terms of new talent. Then they repeat the process with different assumptions to get a sense of how robust the talent predictions are. The executives often decide to adjust their business plans if the associated talent requirements are too great.

Operations managers know that an integral part of managing demand uncertainty is understanding the costs involved in over- or underestimation. But what are the costs of developing too much talent versus too little? Traditionally, workforce planners have implicitly assumed that both the costs and the risks even out: that is, if we forecast we'll need 100 computer programmers in our division next year and we end up with 10 too many or 10 too few, the downsides are the same either way.

In practice, however, that's rarely the case. And, contrary to the situation in the 1950s, the risks of overshooting are greater than those of undershooting, now that workers can leave so easily. If we undershoot, we can always hire on the outside market to make up the difference. The cost per hire will be greater, and so will the uncertainty about employees' abilities, but those costs pale in comparison to retention costs. So, given that the big costs are from overshooting, we will want to develop fewer than 100 programmers and expect to fall somewhat short, hiring on the outside market to make up the difference. If we think our estimate of 100 is reasonably accurate, then perhaps we will want to develop only 90 internally, just to make sure we don't overshoot actual demand, and then plan to hire about 10. If we think our estimate is closer to a guess, we will want to develop fewer, say 60 or so, and plan on hiring the rest outside.

Assessing the trade-offs between making and buying include an educated estimation of the following:

- How long will you need the talent? The longer the talent is needed, the easier it is to make investments in internal development pay off.

- How accurate is your forecast of the length of time you will need the talent? The less certainty about the forecast, the greater the risk and cost of internal development and the greater the appeal of outside hires.

- Is there a hierarchy of skills and jobs that can make it possible for candidates who do not have the requisite competencies to learn them on the job, without resorting to specialized development roles or other costly investments? This is particularly likely in functional areas. The more it is so, the easier it will be to develop talent internally.

- How important is it to maintain the organization's current culture? Especially at the senior level, outside hires introduce different norms and values, changing the culture. If it is important to change the culture, then outside hiring will do that, though sometimes in unpredictable ways.

The answers to these questions may very well be different for different functional areas and jobs within the same company. For instance, lower-level jobs may be easily and cheaply filled by outsiders because the required competencies are readily available, making the costs of undershooting demand relatively modest. For more highly skilled jobs, the costs of undershooting are much higher—requiring the firm to pay for an outside search, a market premium, and perhaps also the costs related to integrating the new hires and absorbing associated risks, such as misfits.

Principle 2: Adapt to the Uncertainty in Talent Demand

If you buy all of your components in bulk and store them away in the warehouse, you are probably buying enough material to produce years of product and therefore have to forecast demand years in advance. But if you bring in small batches of components more often, you don't have to predict demand so far out. The same principle can be applied to shortening the time horizon for talent forecasts in some interesting, and surprisingly simple, ways.

Consider the problem of bringing a new class of candidates into an organization. At companies that hire directly out of college, the entire pool of candidates comes in all at once, typically in June. Let's assume they go through an orientation, spend some time in training classes, and then move into developmental roles. If the new cohort has 100 people, then the organization has to find 100 developmental roles all at once, which can be a challenge for a company under pressure, say, to cut costs or restructure.

But in fact many college graduates don't want to go directly to work after graduation. It's not that difficult to split the new group in half, taking 50 in June and the other 50 in September. Now the program only needs to find 50 roles in June and rotate the new hires through them in three months. The June cohort steps out of those roles when the September cohort steps into them. Then the organization need find only 50 permanent assignments in September for the June hires. More important, having smaller groups of candidates coming through more frequently means that forecasts of demand for these individuals can be made over shorter periods throughout their careers. Not only will those estimates be more accurate but it will be possible to better coordinate the first developmental assignments with subsequent assignments for instance, from test engineer to engineer to senior engineer to lead engineer.

A different way to take advantage of shorter, more responsive forecasts would be to break up a long training program into discrete parts, each with its own forecast. A good place to start would be with the functionally based internal development programs that some companies still offer. These programs often address common subjects, such as general management or interpersonal skills, along with function-specific material. There is no reason that employees in all the functions couldn't go through the general training together and then specialize. What used to be a three-year functional program could become two 18-month courses. After everyone completed the first course, the organization could reforecast the demand for each functional area and allocate the candidates accordingly. Because the functional programs would be half as long, each forecast would only have to go out half as far and would be correspondingly more accurate. An added advantage is that teaching everyone the general skills together reduces redundancy in training investments.

Another risk reduction strategy that talent managers can borrow from supply chain managers is an application of the principle of portfolios. In finance, the problem with holding only one asset is that its value can fluctuate a great deal, and one's wealth varies a lot as a result, so investment advisers remind us to hold several stocks in the same portfolio. Similarly, in supply chain management it can be risky to rely on just one supplier.

For a talent-management application, consider the situation in many large and especially decentralized organizations where each division is accountable for its own profit and loss, and each maintains its own development programs. The odds that any one division will prepare the right number of managers to meet actual demand are very poor. Some will end up with a surplus, others a shortfall. If, however, all of these separate programs were consolidated into a single program, the unanticipated demand in one part of the company and an unanticipated shortfall in another would simply cancel out, just as a stock portfolio reduces the volatility of holding individual stocks. Given this, as well as the duplication of tasks and infrastructure required in decentralized programs, it is a mystery why large organizations continue to operate decentralized development programs. Some companies are in fact creating talent pools that span divisions, developing employees with broad and general competencies that could be applied to a range of jobs. The fit may be less than perfect, but these firms are finding that a little just-in-time training and coaching can help close any gaps.

Principle 3: Improve the Return on Investment in Developing Employees

When internal development was the only way to produce management talent, companies might have been forgiven for paying less attention than they should have to its costs. They may even have been right to consider their expensive development programs as an unavoidable cost of doing business. But the same dynamics that are making today's talent pool less loyal are presenting opportunities for companies to lower the costs of training employees and thereby improve the return on their investment of development dollars, as they might from any R&D effort.

Perhaps the most novel approach to this challenge is to get employees to share in the costs. Since they can cash in on their experience on the open market, employees are the main beneficiaries of their development, so it's reasonable to ask them to contribute. In the United States, legislation prevents hourly workers from having to share in the costs of any training required for their current job. There are no restrictions, however, even for hourly workers, on contributing to the costs of developmental experiences that help prepare employees for future roles.

People might share the costs by taking on learning projects voluntarily, which means doing them in addition to their normal work. Assuming that the candidates are more or less contributing their usual amount to their regular job and their pay hasn't increased, they are essentially doing these development projects for free, no small investment on their part. Pittsburgh-based PNC Financial Services is one of several companies that now offer promising employees the opportunity to volunteer for projects done with the leadership team, sometimes restricting them to ones outside their current functional area. They get access to company leaders, a broadening experience, and good professional contacts, all of which will surely help them later. But they pay for it, with their valuable time.

Employers have been more inclined to experiment with ways to improve the payoff from their development investments by retaining employees longer, or at least for some predictable period. About 20% of U.S. employers ask employees who are about to receive training or development experiences to sign a contract specifying that if they leave the business before a certain time, they will have to pay back the cost. As in the market for carbon credits, this has the effect of putting a monetary value on a previously unaccounted for cost. This practice is especially common in countries like Singapore and Malaysia: Employees often leave anyway, but typically the new employer pays off the old one.

A more interesting practice is to attempt to hang on to employees even after they leave, making relatively small investments in maintaining ties. Deloitte, for example, informs qualified former employees of important developments in the firm and pays the cost of keeping their accounting credentials up-todate. Should these individuals want to switch jobs again, they may well look to the place where they still have ties: Deloitte. And because their skills and company knowledge are current, they will be ready to contribute right away.

Principle 4: Preserve the Investment by Balancing Employee-Employer Interests

The downside of talent portability, of course, is that it makes the fruits of management development perishable in a way they never were in the heyday of the internal development

85

model. It used to be that managers and executives made career decisions for employees, mating individuals and jobs. In the organization-man period, the company would decide which candidates were ready for which experience, in order to meet the longer-term talent needs of the organization. Employees had little or no choice: Refusing to take a new position was a career-ending move.

Today, of course, employees can pick up and leave if they don't get the jobs they want inside—and the most talented among them have the most freedom to do so. In an effort to improve retention, most companies—80% in a recent survey by applicant-tracking company Taleo—have moved away from the chess-master model to internal job boards that make it easy for employees to apply for openings and so change jobs within the organization. Dow Chemical, for example, cut its turnover rate in half when it moved its vacancies to such internal boards.

These arrangements have effectively turned the problem of career management over to employees. As a result,employers have much less control over their internal talent. Employees' choices may not align with the interests of the employer, and internal conflicts are increasing because half of the employers in the U.S. no longer require that employees seek permission from their supervisors to move to new positions.

So it has become imperative for companies to find more effective ways to preserve their management development investment. The key is to negotiate solutions that balance the interests of all parties. McKinsey's arrangement for associates relies not only on how they rank their preferences for projects posted online but also on how the principals running the projects rank the associates. The final decision allocating resources is made by a senior partner who tries to honor the preferences of both sides while choosing the assignment that will best develop the skill set of each associate. Bear, Stearns established an office of mediation, which negotiates internal disputes between managers when an employee wants to move from one job to another in the firm.

The talent problems of employers, employees, and the broader society are intertwined. Employers want the skills they need when they need them, delivered in a manner they can afford. Employees want prospects for advancement and control over their careers. The societies in which they operate and the economy as a whole need higher levels of skills— particularly deeper competencies in management—which are best developed inside companies.

Those often-conflicting desires aren't addressed by existing development practices. The language and the frameworks of the organization-man model persist despite the fact that few companies actually employ it; there simply aren't any alternatives. The language comes from engineering and is rooted in the idea that we can achieve certainty through planning—an outdated notion. But before an old paradigm can be overthrown there must be an alternative, one that describes new challenges better than the old one can. If the language of the old paradigm was dominated by engineering and planning, the language of the new, talent-on-demand framework is driven by markets and operations-based tools better suited to the challenges of uncertainty. Talent on demand gives employers a way to manage their talent needs and recoup investments in development, a way to balance the interests of employees and employers, and a way to increase the level of skills in society.

The Idea in Brief

Operations Principles Applied to Talent Management

A supply chain perspective on talent management relies on four principles, two that address the risks in estimating demand and two that address the uncertainty of supply.

Principle 1: Make *and* Buy to Manage Risk

A deep bench of talent is expensive, so companies should undershoot their estimates of what will be needed and plan to hire from outside to make up for any shortfall. Some positions may be easier to fill from outside than others, so firms should be thoughtful about where they put precious resources in development: Talent management is an investment, not an entitlement.

Principle 2: Adapt to the Uncertainty in Talent Demand

Uncertainty in demand is a given, and smart companies find ways to adapt to it. One approach is to break up development programs into shorter units: Rather than put management trainees through a three-year functional program, for instance, bring employees from all the functions together in an 18-month course that teaches general management skills, and then send them back to their functions to specialize. Another option is to create an organization-wide talent pool that can be allocated among business units as the need arises.

Principle 3: Improve the Return on Investment in Developing Employees

One way to improve the payoff is to get employees to share in the costs of development. That might mean asking them to take on additional stretch assignments on a volunteer basis. Another approach is to maintain relationships with former employees in the hope that they may return someday, bringing back your investment in their skills.

Principle 4: Preserve the Investment by Balancing Employee-Employer Interests

Arguably, the main reason good employees leave an organization is that they find better opportunities elsewhere. This makes talent development a perishable commodity. The key to preserving your investment in development efforts as long as possible is to balance the interests of employees and employer by having them share in advancement decisions

---

.